EVALUATING FEDERAL SOCIAL PROGRAMS

An Uncertain Art

Sar A. Levitan
and
Gregory K. Wurzburg

September 1979

THE W. E. UPJOHN INSTITUTE FOR EMPLOYMENT RESEARCH

Library of Congress Cataloging in Publication Data

Levitan, Sar A
  Evaluating Federal social programs.

  Includes bibliographical references and index.
    1. Evaluation research (Social action programs)—
United States.   I. Wurzburg, Gregory, joint author.
II. Title.
H62.5.U5L47   362'.973   79-17946
ISBN   0-911558-64-0 (paper)
ISBN   0-911558-65-9 (cloth)

THE INSTITUTE, a nonprofit research organization, was established on July 1, 1945. It is an activity of the W. E. Upjohn Unemployment Trustee Corporation, which was formed in 1932 to administer a fund set aside by the late Dr. W. E. Upjohn for the purpose of carrying on "research into the causes and effects of unemployment and measures for the alleviation of unemployment."

This study is for sale by the Institute at $3.50 per copy for paperback and $5.50 per copy for cloth cover. For quantity orders of this publication or any combination of Institute publications, price reductions are as follows: 10-25 copies, 10 percent; 26-50, 15; 51-100, 20; over 100, 25.

iii

Foreword

Expanded needs for information that can be used to measure the effects of a broad array of social programs have occurred as a result of the federal government's increased social policy role during the past two decades. During this period, evaluation of the efficiency and effectiveness of federal social programs has been related increasingly to the policy formulation process. Within the federal government, agencies' responsibilities for program evaluation have increased rapidly in response to congressional requirements for the assessment of the impacts of major social legislative initiatives.

This study assesses the current state of the art of both process and impact evaluation, with emphasis on the limitations of evaluation tools currently in use. Levitan and Wurzburg also have provided an in-depth analysis of the federal government's institutional arrangements and process for evaluating social programs. The need for evaluation and the use of best available evaluation methodologies are clearly recognized by the authors. However, Levitan and Wurzburg detail serious limitations of both evaluation tools and institutional arrangements for federal social program evaluation. The study is published with the expectation that the authors' critique of social program evaluation will contribute to informed discussion and ultimate improvements in program evaluation as an important tool for planning and public policy development.

The facts presented in this study and the observations and viewpoints expressed are the sole responsibility of the authors. They do not necessarily represent positions of the W. E. Upjohn Institute for Employment Research.

E. Earl Wright
Director

Kalamazoo, Michigan
September 1979

v

The Authors

SAR A. LEVITAN is Research Professor of Economics and director of the Center for Social Policy Studies at The George Washington University. He is also chairman of the National Commission on Employment and Unemployment Statistics. He has been a consultant to various governmental agencies and has served on labor panels for the Federal Mediation and Conciliation Service and the American Arbitration Association. Included among the many books he has authored or coauthored are *Programs in Aid of the Poor for the 1970s; The Great Society's Poor Law; Work is Here to Stay, Alas; Human Resources and Labor Markets; The Promise of Greatness; Shorter Hours, Shorter Weeks: Spreading the Work to Reduce Unemployment; Warriors at Work; The Volunteer Armed Force;* and *More Than Subsistence: Minimum Wages for the Working Poor.*

GREGORY K. WURZBURG is executive director of the National Council on Employment Policy and a former research associate with the Center for Social Policy Studies, The George Washington University.

Preface

Federal programs in the United States are under continuous scrutiny, and some have been subject to sustained attack. Advocates of an activist federal role are on the defensive, realizing that the era of rapid growth of both the economy and social programs has halted for the time being. Retrenchment in certain areas is even likely. Although the citizenry continues to clamor for new forms of federal assistance, the realities of the vast American production machine require at least selective slowdowns in the rate of growth. Sound management may even require outright curtailment of some efforts. If society cannot afford to support all the existing social programs, the challenge before policymakers is to select the likely candidates for cut-backs, and improve those that remain.

In a broad sense, the need is to establish a mechanism to permit rational allocation of resources. There is an increasing demand to know what past spending has accomplished and where future spending will produce the biggest bang for the buck. Policymakers have, therefore, turned to the modern day wisemen for help in divining the means to determine which programs are to be axed and which should be continued or even expanded.

There is no record that the founding fathers were directly concerned with problems of evaluating social programs—there was precious little to evaluate. But the system they designed is admirably suited for obtaining, in the end, sufficient evidence for policymakers to draw informed conclusions about the effectiveness of federal efforts. The separation of the three branches of government, particularly the executive and legislative, permits, indeed encourages, independent evaluation of social programs. While Congress has been slow in seizing the opportunity to obtain independent assessment of the programs, it is rapidly establishing a network that feeds back information about the impact of the multitude of efforts that it has mandated. The executive branch, in even greater need of scrutinizing the operation and impact of social programs because it has the direct responsibility for implementing and administering these efforts, has been established in the business for years. But the potential role of evaluation in a system of checks and balances has not been fully realized.

This study examines the tools that evaluators have developed to practice their trade and reviews the institutional arrangements that have been devised for the care and nourishment of the evaluators. The volume also assesses the comparative strengths and weaknesses of the evaluation establishments in the two branches of government. It concentrates especially on the programs assigned to the Department of Health, Education and Welfare and the Department of Labor, the two major federal agencies responsible for administering social measures and the principal source of insights for policymaking in both branches.

Arguing that it is better to make decisions on the basis of the best available information (although not denying the dangers of only a little knowledge), the authors question whether the tools available to evaluators and the climate in which they work permit them to design objective criteria and valid and reliable methods. The central issue for scrutiny is whether evaluation as it is practiced provides a convincing basis for making decisions about social programs.

Federal programs offer a comprehensive system of social services for Americans. This federal role evolved as a product of a normative process, an expression of what *ought to be*. The authors conclude that it is highly questionable whether evaluators can provide a new, precise calculus capable of changing that situation. In the final analysis, no matter how sophisticated and careful the evaluation of social programs may be, value judgments and political considerations remain paramount, controlling the decisions made by policymakers.

But hope springs eternal. Congress keeps asking for more and appropriates the funds to assure the delivery of new evaluations, while officials in the executive branch pay lip service to the evaluation of their programs. There is little evidence, however, that much use is made of the products.

For the purpose of this study, evaluation is broadly defined to include the presentation of evidence on program performance and its impact. The reader will obviously note that this definition does not attempt to pinpoint what constitutes relevant evidence. That's why a whole book is needed on the subject, and a definition will not do.

An earlier draft of the study was completed more than a year ago but its publication was deferred due to pressures of other responsibilities. Meanwhile, the draft received rather wide circulation among evaluators—inside and outside government—beyond the expectations of the authors. The agonizing attacks persuaded us that the study is on the mark and that it might be of interest to a wider audience.

We are grateful to our not very admiring critics. Their attacks helped improve our product, but they are, of course, absolved from any of the remaining transgressions. In addition to Harold Orlans, who offered painstaking and valuable criticisms and suggestions, we are also indebted to Henry Aaron, Gregory Ahart, Burt Barnow, Michael Borus, Seymour Brandwein, Peter Henle, Joseph Hight, Robert Levine, Arnold Packer, Howard Rosen, Fred Siskind, Ernst Stromsdorfer, and Barry White for their helpful written comments. The names of critics supplying oral comments, no matter how forcefully presented, are omitted, though their observations were carefully noted. The authors also thank Nancy Kiefer for seeing the manuscript through its iterations and preparing it for publication.

This study was prepared under a grant from The Ford Foundation to The George Washington University's Center for Social Policy Studies. In accordance with the Foundation's practice, responsibility for the content was left completely to the authors.

Sar A. Levitan
Gregory Wurzburg

Washington, DC
September 1979

ix

Contents

1

The Aspirations and Limitations of Evaluators

IN PURSUIT OF SOME UNCERTAINTY

Much of our social policy has been undertaken on faith. Education, established early as a good that should be available to, and indeed forced on, all children, has yet to prove its intrinsic value. Nonetheless, it is considered almost unpatriotic to question that commitment. Once social security became law, it successfully withstood attacks on its basic underpinnings because of the popularity of a nation-wide system of social insurance. The validity of a federal role encouraging home ownership and providing shelter for low-income families, also remains strong after more than forty years.

In the 1960s, however, the federal government's role in the social policy arena departed dramatically from historical patterns, raising questions and demanding justification. The federal government was moving into policy areas that traditionally had been the domain of states or private organizations. In particular, the increased federal role in education and public welfare sparked debate on some fundamental questions of federalism. When the federal government entered new fields that no level of government had seriously considered before, there was further controversy about the limits of governmental responsibility. The reactivation of New Deal concepts of economic development, community development, and manpower development after three decades was

1

viewed by some critics as a dangerous incursion, threatening to private sector opportunities. Targeted programs and civil rights laws aimed at providing compensatory services to the poor raised the ire of people who had mistaken the rhetoric of equal opportunity and equal justice for all, for reality. In this charged atmosphere of social change, inquiries about which programs worked, why they worked, and how they could be improved were inevitable. Advocates of the new federal activism looked to evaluations for evidence to defend their case. The detractors sought ammunition to wage the battle against what they viewed as conceptually unsound and administratively unworkable social initiatives.

Even before the social programs of the Great Society moved center stage, another essential force was carving out a niche for evaluators in the federal bureaucracy. In an attempt to introduce some order into the processes of policy analysis and decision-making, Robert McNamara, Secretary for Defense under Presidents Kennedy and Johnson, applied a systems approach entitled the Programming, Planning, and Budgeting System (PPBS) to the review of that agency's missions. President Johnson then foisted PPBS on other federal agencies. Evaluation came to be viewed as part of the "feedback loop" whose assessments would be an essential ingredient of the policy formulation process.

PPBS was neither as successful nor as popular as its architects had hoped it would be. It failed to impose much order on the management process and had little apparent effect on improving the work of civilian agencies. But it did leave a legacy expressed in the lingering notion that evaluation, research, and analysis, if done correctly, could supply needed guides to policymakers. Indeed, the most enthusiastic proponents of PPBS endorsed it as a *deus ex machina* capable even of making decisions for the mortal administrator.

THE APPLICATION OF EVALUATION

The growing need for information about the effects of Washington's bold new policies coupled with the magical powers bestowed on evaluation by the PPBS movement significantly legitimized the role of evaluation in the policy formulation process. The evaluation trade has continued to flourish since the early 1960s. Most federal agencies having responsibilities for social programs maintain sizeable budgets for program assessment activities. Congress writes evaluation requirements into virtually all new social legislation. According to one estimate by the Office of Management and Budget, about $140 million was spent in 1978 for evaluating federal social programs.

The multitude of evaluations are undertaken in the name of providing information to legislators, administrators, and the general public. The main questions they are designed to answer are whether to retain a program, change its level of funding, or modify its objectives or the strategies for achieving those objectives.

Despite their broadening scope, evaluations have not succeeded in dispelling doubts, nor have they lent much order to the process by which social policy is formulated. Notwithstanding the appeal of evaluation to policymakers, the actual connection between evaluation and policy formulation is attentuated. In the final analysis, there is still a mismatch between what evaluators have to say, and what policymakers and the public need to know.

The reasons for the meager payoffs of evaluation are not hard to fathom. The most basic deficiency is simply that the meaning and purpose of evaluation are fuzzy. To paraphrase Alice's Mad Hatter—evaluation means exactly what anyone may want it to mean. Webster is concise in defining evaluation: "to find the value or amount of." But this definition provides few guidelines for most people who bandy the term to serve their own needs. For the government bureaucrat, the term may trigger an alarm because "evaluation" is perceived as a threat to the agency's programs. Members of Congress may use the term as a political tool, while the practitioner of the trade may perceive evaluation as an exercise by an impartial observer to gain insights about a program.

Whatever the definition of the term, its meaning is not clarified by the attempts of evaluators to impose rationality upon various applications of the concept. Some evaluations are narrow inquiries into programs that have been hastily designed to respond to complex problems and whose impacts cannot be isolated from other developments. Furthermore, the laws authorizing social programs are filled with conflicting goals and vague specifications for program results that are frequently non-observable, non-quantifiable, or otherwise difficult to gauge. Even where hard data can be obtained, standards for judging performance are often arbitrary.

Amassing knowledge to evaluate the efficiency and effectiveness of social programs also has inherent drawbacks. There is a misplaced confidence in the assumption that social problems and governmental solutions have a continuity that allows lessons gleaned from observing them to be stacked like bricks. Social, political, and economic conditions are ever-changing, and program responses are altered almost as frequently. It is misleading and presumptuous on the part of social scientists to create simplistic models of program objectives and effects, pretending there is order where little exists. The consequences of these conceptual shortcomings to evaluation are predictable and dismaying: evaluators encourage, and policymakers too readily accept, social policies predicated on fragmented views of social problems and the effect of social change. The policies reflect a mechanical internal consistency that flies in the face of reason, where common sense dictates a holistic and judgmental approach.

State-of-the-art limitations are not the only restraint on the usefulness of social program evaluations. The process is flawed frequently by evaluators overselling their products and urging excessive reliance on their findings and conclusions. Policymakers, eager to shift their burden of responsibility to mechanical decision models, are only too ready to accept the snake oil remedies uncritically. Administrative obstacles also limit the potential usefulness of evaluation. Policy designers and program administrators frequently demand instant assessments of intricate problems without adequately considering the perspective from which evaluations are undertaken or the appropriate means of procuring evaluation services. And some evaluators always stand ready to supply quickie products that are inaccurate and cast doubt upon the reliability of all evaluators. Related to this is the difficulty of securing independent evaluators who are willing to deliver conclusions based on best available facts no matter how unfavorable the message may be to the sponsors.

The limited effectiveness of evaluation has prompted some predictable reactions. Congress interprets these shortcomings as arising from administrators' reluctance to use the available tools. Consequently, it mandates more evaluations with each passing year, shifting the requirements as to who should do the evaluation and how they should do it. Meanwhile, evaluation administrators often pursue their own agendas unmindful of larger program objectives and agency missions. Other managers, lamenting what they perceive to be meager gains from evaluation activities, attempt to improve the yield by tinkering with the way evaluation is managed. In the mid-1970s, the Office of Management and Budget (OMB) tried to establish some norms for administering evaluation. OMB was no more successful than others in clearly defining the scope of evaluation, and its muscle in the executive establishment offered a poor substitute for intellectual substance. Not to be deterred by OMB's failure, the General Accounting Office began in 1976 a more modest project that was still aimed at standardizing management of evaluation—first in the Department of Housing and Urban Development and then in the Department of Labor. Its early results look no more promising than those of OMB.

Legislators and administrators have been joined in the general attempt to improve the productivity and end product of evaluators. Academics and technicians have intensified their search for the Holy Grail, attempting to invigorate the evaluation trade by upgrading methodologies. In their labors, they try to identify critical variables, fashion control groups, and collect data that will provide answers to questions raised in the search for solutions. But while they have been improving the sophistication and elegance of their tools, the new methodologies appear as flawed as simple efforts of the past. The added mountains of data are more neatly arranged and tabulated, but definitive information on bothersome policy issues remains elusive. Social inquiry is being steered, increasingly, by the methodological tools available, not by the fundamental questions being asked. Where the methodologies should be providing broader, more balanced pictures, they are focusing more and more on the fragments that yield to quantitative measures and analysis, inducing policymakers to focus their attention on the trees, and lose sight of the forest. Neither do the new methodologies provide better answers to the central questions of what evaluation should accomplish and what role it rightfully deserves in policy design and formulation. There is a surreal quality to these efforts as the social scientists attempt to improve even more their techniques for counting the number of angels that can dance on the head of a pin.

FLAWS IN THE FOUNDATION

The development of social program evaluation resembles an evangelical movement. The surge in social spending in the 1960s spawned the conditions and generated support for evaluations. It may well be that the only way evaluation could gain recognition as a major policy tool was by coming in with great fanfare. But money alone does not create ideas—the movement lacked the glue of rationality from the beginning. Consequently, the legacy of that dramatic entrance is a weak foundation buckling under the pressure of proponents attempting indiscriminately to push evaluation beyond its capabilities.

The foundation for the evaluation of social programs was weakened from the beginning by a number of flawed assumptions. The most deficient was held by social scientists who asserted that systematic inquiry could successfully disaggregate social problems into discrete packages treatable with individual policy prescriptions. Another underlying weakness was the belief held by social scientists and evaluators that if more accurate and reliable information were available, legislators and administrators would use it as a basis for enacting and implementing legislation. Third, evaluators, trusting the power of their tools, presumed themselves able to identify important program variables in a real-life setting and to isolate and describe changes induced by policy. In short, all three flaws have reflected perverse positivism—perhaps an inevitable by-product of the success of the scientific method in pushing technology. Their impact has been to upset the balance between subjective judgment and empirical observation, with more reliance placed on the latter and less on the former.

The evaluation establishment has also fallen prey to serious shortcomings. Because of noncomparability among efforts, isolated and frequently conflicting findings from individual programs cannot be cumulated or woven together well enough to form the solid base of experience advocated by evaluation promoters. Differing assumptions have also muddied the waters. Instead of the sensitivity needed to trace the development of social science knowledge from disparate pieces of information, there have been impatience and immodest expectations.[1]

THE LIMITED POTENTIAL

Flawed assumptions have severely diminished the utility of evaluation as a tool for policy analysis. But these same assumptions form the basis for a great deal of today's social science. Therefore, a critique of the federal government's social program evaluation policy confined to that approach is doomed to an uphill struggle and runs the risk of stressing issues not central to evaluation.

It is valuable instead to focus specifically on the mechanisms and institutional arrangements for evaluation. That is where it is most clearly identified as a "discipline" separate from social science. That is where evaluation is most susceptible to change. And that is where our critique can be related to the broader, more systemic features of social inquiry.

The authors are not arguing that evaluation fails to teach any lessons. But there are limits to what even the most conclusive findings can imply for future policy. When those limits are ignored, the potential for abuse is enormous, the possible consequence costly, and misguided conclusions may put in jeopardy the stability of society.

1. Henry J. Aaron, *Politics and the Professors* (Washington: The Brookings Institution, 1978), pp. 146-167.

2
Tools of the Trade

STATE OF THE ART

Evaluating the federal government's social initiatives is more art than science. The programs, even in their conception, are imprecise tools for intervention. They frequently approach the problems they are meant to solve from an oblique angle, and provide only partial solutions. Valid and realistic standards for judging them are critically lacking. Implemented in an environment charged with emotional and political disagreement and subject to a number of uncontrollable variables, the programs defy careful and systematic evaluation.

The tools available for evaluating the programs are crude. In the words of one federal evaluation administrator, "We are almost pre-Copernican in our understanding of the social science methodology in this area."[1] The conditions under which evaluators operate make even the semblance of a scientific methodology impractical. Evaluators are rarely in the position to design programs in such a way as to provide adequate tests for important elements. Claims about the ability to observe results—directly or through proxy measures—are frequently pretentious. The notion of achieving experimental conditions, so

---

1. William Morrill, *Government Economy and Spending Reform Act of 1976,* Hearings before U.S. Congress, Senate Committee on Government Operations (Washington: Government Printing Office, 1976), pp. 443-465.

9

central to scientific inquiry, is a virtually unattainable ideal. An enormous number of variables influencing any program are beyond the control of even the most imaginative and powerful policymaker, to say nothing of a lowly evaluator. Yet, in spite of the difficulties of even crude scientific inquiry, policymakers demand assessments of social programs, and evaluators respond, cranking them out with a vengeance.

Hoping to bring to their professions a degree of credibility that the substance of their work sometimes fails to provide, evaluators have collected an impressive array of tools for their trade. Although the collection may seem to border on witchcraft, it is intended to impart a sense of rigorous and systematic inquiry.

Ultimately, the methodology that evaluators adopt is shaped by the decisionmakers' inquiries and the likely applications they will make of the findings. At different levels of decisionmaking, different issues assume prominence. Program operators zero in on program management and logistics, while the bottom line for legislators is the difference a program makes. Between these two extremes are many intermediate interests and decision points that reflect complexities of the social programs themselves, and of their interaction with the world.

Although the questions of decisionmakers do not fall into neat pigeonholes, and the evaluations designed to provide the answers are often less than tidy, the general methodological approaches that form the basis of any inquiry can be broken into two genres: process evaluations and impact evaluations. The first assesses whether a program is a workable tool for change, and the second assesses the effects of a program in achieving the desired change. The focuses of the two approaches differ dramatically, as do their respective methodological strategies.

Assessing Workability: Process Evaluations

Whether a program effectively attacks a social problem is of secondary concern to the administrator whose prime task is to implement the program. Will unemployed veterans enroll in training courses for auto mechanics? Who will seek services from a community health center and what number of clients will strain existing facilities? In assessing workability, the evaluator focuses on how faithfully intervention tools implied in policy mandates have been implemented.

The scope of a process evaluation is confined to assessing what a particular program has accomplished in meeting its immediate objectives, and assessing the "workability" of a program. Process evaluations take as their starting point the presumption that a program is conceptually sound, and focus on the evaluation of "effort," including administrative practices, staffing patterns, caseloads, and unit costs.[2] Without such evidence, it is difficult for policymakers and other evaluation users to distinguish between failures caused by process insufficiencies (lack of trained staff or inappropriate target groups, for example) and impact-related program design flaws (e.g., no relation between training and employment). Edward Suchman identified four dimensions of social intervention strategies more suited for separate process evaluation than for analysis of program impact.[3]

Operational elements are critical first determinants of success or failure. Decisionmaking structures, political interactions, staff competence, the physical condition of facilities, financial management practices, and the level of supportive services all play a part in how effectively a program concept is implemented. Although the concern is not with measuring program results, process evaluations can imply as much about program success as can impact studies. Operational elements are as important an influence as program strategy in the pursuit of immediate program objectives and long range results. An analysis of the public Employment Service found personal leadership and political support to have important effects on the success of the agency's programs.[4] Studies of implementation of the Comprehensive

2. Joseph S. Wholey, *et al.*, *Federal Evaluation Policy* (Washington: The Urban Institute, 1973), pp. 95-96.

3. Edward Suchman, *Evaluative Research: Principles and Practices in Public Service and Social Action Programs* (New York: Russell Sage Foundation, 1967), pp. 64-69.

4. Mark L. Chadwin, *et al.*, *The Employment Service: An Institutional Analysis* (Washington: Government Printing Office, 1977).

Employment and Training Act and of local management of employment and training programs have shown clear links between operations and program results.[5]

It is also important to know precisely who is being served. This is especially significant in the case of most federal social programs because the intended beneficiaries of the programs normally have little political clout; consequently, there has always been the concern that persons with less need would benefit from the programs. Since resources are limited, administrators must establish priorities and choose to serve only part of the target population. "Disadvantaged youth," for instance, is a group that encompasses more persons than Congress ever envisioned in designing the several youth programs to serve them. The choice of which subsections to serve is an important determinant of what a program does, how it operates, and what it finally achieves. The evaluator has to specify, even if the administrator has failed to do so, who is being served by a particular program. To do otherwise may hinder an accurate interpretation of the results.

The third dimension of process evaluation concerns the environmental conditions under which a program operates. Knowledge about them is useful for determining whether or not the lessons learned from a program are transferable. Generalizations about what does and does not work must be made with an understanding of the qualities that are inherent in a program design as contrasted with outside factors that impact upon the program.

The final dimension of process evaluation is the determination of whether a program succeeds as an intervention tool in achieving its immediate objectives. Do those who complete a training program acquire a saleable skill? Do rehabilitation programs leave enrollees in a position to compete in the job market? Assessing these proximate results, however, is not the same as assessing effectiveness. For example, the Elementary and Secondary Education Act of 1965 succeeded in channeling more education

---

5. Randall Ripley, *CETA Prime Sponsor Management Decisions and Program Goal Achievement* (Washington: Government Printing Office, 1978).

funds to schools with high concentrations of children from low-income families and in boosting outlays per low-income pupil. But the effectiveness of that strategy in equalizing education opportunities or in equalizing academic achievement for low-income groups remains unproven.[6] Similarly, the Youth Employment and Demonstration Projects Act of 1977 succeeded in prodding local manpower and education administrators to work on joint projects, but it is still unclear whether increased cooperation has brought about increased employability opportunities for youth.[7]

Gauging Results: Impact Evaluation

In contrast to the narrow scope of process evaluation, program impact evaluation attempts to examine accomplishments and therefore has broader appeal.

Underlying the analysis of program impact is the hope that the investigators can find out which tactics work and how successful the programs utilizing them have been. In a controlled environment where the only variable would be the program being tested, isolating the differences attributable to it would be a simple task. In the case of employment and training programs designed to increase employability and raise earnings, comparisons could presumably be drawn between employment rates and income levels before and after the program. To determine if education finance programs had equalized per pupil expenditures, educators might look for increases in academic achievement among students in poorer schools.

The environment in which the evaluator of social programs functions, however, is not controlled. Unknown, uncontrollable, and unpredictable forces are at work. Trying to estimate what would have happened in the absence of the program and inferring its impact are frustrating experiences. In the employment and training arena, changes over time in labor demand, wage levels,

6. Sar A. Levitan and Robert Taggart, *The Promise of Greatness* (Cambridge, MA: Harvard University Press, 1976), p. 119.

7. Gregory Wurzburg, "Improving Job Opportunities for Youth," National Council on Employment Policy, 1978, pp. 45-49.

and the structural composition of the work force can distort or mask the effects of government intervention. Eligibility criteria and benefit levels, which vary widely among states, influence client response to changes in welfare programs. Measurement problems also cause difficulties; valid, reliable, and accurate social indicators are rare, and precision is illusory much of the time.

In real life, measures of the effects of social programs are relative, not absolute. The evaluator's only choice is to control the nonprogram variables as much as possible in attempting to isolate the change caused by the program. The designs that have been developed vary in their complexity, the presumption being that greater sophistication of the research design improves the chances of isolating and estimating the impacts that programs have on client groups.[8]

More sophisticated designs are inevitably more costly though, in terms of time, money, and flexibility. Steep tradeoffs and relatively low marginal yields on increasingly sophisticated evaluative designs make the most sophisticated modes the exception rather than the rule.

IT'S NOT THAT SIMPLE

Evaluators might reach a consensus about objectives of different approaches to solving social problems. But in the process of designing even the simplest evaluation, the choice of variables to be tested, participants to be observed, and indicators to employ as measures of progress, are explicitly or implicitly a matter of judgment. Yet those subjective judgments determine the kind of data that will be collected, and affect the conclusions that may be derived from them. Not merely incidental qualifications attached to certain conclusions, these subjective judgments impose fundamental constraints on what can be inferred validly from the evidence produced by evaluations.

Evaluation methodologists are fond of asserting that the barriers to objective evaluations could be removed if only there

---

8. Suchman, *op. cit.*

were clearer specification of goals and objectives, improved access to available data, and a larger role for evaluators in program design and administration. The U.S. General Accounting Office criticized the evaluation system in the Department of Housing and Urban Development because policy officials were not effectively communicating program goals to evaluators, and because the goals were not quantified.[9] Too frequently, evaluators have stubbornly refused to recognize or acknowledge that methodological and administrative impediments to evaluation are not a function of intractable program operators or legislative vagaries but, rather, are intimately linked to the very nature of social programs.

Usually, neither the laws authorizing national social programs nor the agencies charged with implementing them are explicit about what they want to do. The old adage, "when you don't know where you're going, any road will get you there," applies frequently in this sphere because lawmakers find it convenient not to spell out their real intentions.

Title XX of the Social Security Act is a case in point. The Act authorizes grants to states for social services "[to encourage] each state . . . to furnish services directed to the goal of achieving or maintaining economic self-support to prevent, reduce, or eliminate dependency. . . ." The legislation offers no guidance as to who the legislation is aimed at, what outputs might be expected, or what the intermediate objectives might be. Little more is offered to the project designers. Indeed, the evaluator would have a difficult time determining reasonable criteria for judging achievement or output. Liberals found the notion of federal support for social services attractive. Conservatives got the language they favored, and none of the parties involved seemed to have any qualms about saddling Uncle Sam with the payments for various social services. None championed spelling out the appropriate services and client eligibility criteria.

There are obvious cases where objectives are intentionally made ambiguous in order to draw broad and multifaceted support for

---

9. Comptroller General of the United States, *HUD's Evaluation System: An Assessment* (Washington: General Accounting Office, 1978), pp. ii, 39.

the legislation. Various groups have often supported the same broad goals for different, and sometimes even conflicting, reasons. Charles L. Schultze cites the Elementary and Secondary Education Act of 1965 as an example of "legislative pluralism" in which a law was able to pass because the objectives were sufficiently vague to attract the support of diverse interest groups. According to his analysis, this law gained the support of a coalition of three groups that, separately, could not have exerted sufficient pressure to achieve passage: parochial school interests, advocates of federal aid to education, and antipoverty warriors. To avoid offending any partner, the designers of the legislation used sufficiently nebulous objectives to attract maximum support without alienating any participating group.[10] The law declared that "The policy of the United States [is] to provide financial assistance . . . to meeting special educational needs of educationally deprived children." Any evaluator would find it difficult to gauge the performance of a program in terms of the "objectives" of the Act. Given this noble purpose, there would also be very little that any legislator's constituents would find particularly offensive. However, it would also offer very little to the evaluator trying to establish more scientific objectives as a basis for assessing program performance.

Even where evaluators find themselves reviewing programs with well-specified objectives and quantifiable goals and their immediate tasks become somewhat easier, the challenge to do a worthwhile assessment of a particular program and to have an impact on policy does not diminish. For example, the Youth Employment and Demonstration Projects Act of 1977 spelled out legislative objectives in great detail. Those objectives were augmented by the Department of Labor. However, whether federal officials will be in a position to evaluate the program with any greater precision than if the laws were vague about its objective is no certainty. Among other factors, demographic changes in the 1980s, or the renewal of a military draft may

---

10. Charles L. Schultze, *The Politics and Economics of Public Spending* (Washington: The Brookings Institution, 1968), pp. 47-49.

completely overhaul programs under the Act and, consequently, alter the task of the evaluators.[11]

Goals, objectives, and purposes that are articulated in legislation do not represent inviolable verities, but merely a consensus of what is desirable and feasible at one point in time. The social environment, perceptions of needs, and impacts of the programs are continually changing. Numerous external forces are not foreseeable at the legislative stage. "Evaluators with their attention concentrated on declared objectives may overlook unexpected results of equal or greater value."[12] Furthermore, neat statements of objectives do not always reflect the priorities and policies of a federal agency or of legislative sponsors. Hidden agendas and non-specified political objectives are often as high a priority to decisionmakers as stated design objectives. In addition, spillover effects and unanticipated interactions and developments in the program environment may significantly affect what the programs accomplish, as well as the implications of particular program results.[13]

To the extent that evaluators confine their perspectives to these narrow objectives stated for public consumption and for history to record, they can lay claim to building a degree of objectivity into their work. It is almost certain that a like-minded evaluator, guided by the spirit of scientific method, could replicate the approach, but the cost would be steep. Their revisions are doomed to be sterile works marked by slavish internal consistency, but with little relevance to the needs of policymakers having to make choices in the real world.

A potentially valuable alternative is a much more problematical approach in which evaluators' perceptions of the program goals

---

11. Office of Youth Programs, "A Planning Charter for the Youth Employment and Demonstration Projects Act of 1977," U.S. Department of Labor, August 1977.

12. Garth Mangum and John Walsh, *Employment and Training Programs for Youth: What Works Best for Whom?* (Washington: Government Printing Office, 1978), p. 53.

13. Carol H. Weiss, "Where Politics and Evaluation Research Meet," *Evaluation,* Vol. 1, No. 3, 1973; and Michael E. Borus and William R. Tash, *Measuring the Impact of Manpower Programs: A Primer* (Ann Arbor: Institute of Labor and Industrial Relations, University of Michigan-Wayne State University, 1970).

would replace the formal legislative intent. A useful and intelligent evaluation of the impact of social programs has to be more than a mechanical comparison of what was formally attempted and actually accomplished. Moreover, insistence on methodological rigor may exclude information that cannot be incorporated in a tidy research design but that is vital to understanding policy issues. Evaluation research should be flexible enough to permit redefinition of the objectives and issues it addresses. Social programs function in changing environments, and the standards used for judging them should reflect these changes. Granted, evaluation may become more art than science, but, more important, it would become a better mirror of reality.

WHAT IS AN APPROPRIATE INDICATOR?

The selection of indicators for measuring the accomplishments of social programs can be another significant source of distortion. This process is intrinsic to the choice of goals and objectives, and no less vulnerable to institutional and state-of-the-art constraints. In the jargon of the trade, indicators must meet tests of validity and reliability and they should reflect substantive change caused by the program being evaluated.[14] The problems associated with the unemployment rate and crime index illuminate the difficulties of measuring different aspects of social well-being.

The unemployment rate is a mainstay for identifying labor market pathologies and economic malaise. Yet it is a misleading indicator of social and economic welfare because it does not fully reflect the problems of underemployment and inadequate earnings that are at least as relevant as unemployment in ascertaining overall social and economic welfare.[15] Even as a limited purpose indicator, however, it is deficient. Measurement problems plague the current standards and frequently they are neither accurate nor reliable.[16]

14. Suchman, *op. cit.*

15. Sar A. Levitan and Robert Taggart, *Employment and Earnings Inadequacy: A New Social Indicator* (Baltimore: The Johns Hopkins University Press, 1974).

16. The National Commission on Employment and Unemployment Statistics, *Counting the Labor Force,* a draft prepared for public comment (Washington: Government Printing Office, 1979), Ch. 3.

The U.S. crime index suffers from lack of credibility because it does not reflect the public's notion of crime.[17] It is also vulnerable to variations in unstandardized data collection procedures. Failing to weight for different kinds of crime, and going for more than 44 years without adjustments for changes in demographics or changes in prices, the index has outlived any usefulness it may have had.

Most critical indicators used in evaluation are less global in their concerns than unemployment measures or the crime index. They still fall victim, however, to some flaws. More directly program-related is the recent Department of Health, Education and Welfare campaign to encourage motorcyclists to wear safety helmets. The measure of program effectiveness selected was the change in the number of motorcyclist fatalities. Analysts hoped to establish a causal link between the number of motorcyclists wearing helmets and the number of lives saved.[18] However, HEW evaluators attributed all of the subsequent drop in motorcyclists' fatalities to the program and conveniently disregarded factors unrelated to the safety program that might have contributed to the decline in fatalities.

In the Department of Labor's Employment and Training Administration, officials adopted 13 indicators to assess the ongoing effectiveness of local program administrators' performance. The quarterly indicators measured performance with respect to unit cost, proportion of participants placed in unsubsidized jobs, and post-program earnings. It was presumed that a high score would correlate with positive long term program effects such as increased earning power and enhanced employability for participants. While this choice of indicators is appealing as a measure of good management, it does not appear to be a very good predictor of program impact. Analysis has shown there to be very little relationship between what the indicators show a

17. Judith Ann deNeufville, *Social Indicators and Social Policy* (New York: Elsevier Scientific Publishing Co., 1975), pp. 101-119.

18. Harley Hinrichs and Graeme Taylor, *Program Budgeting and Benefit Cost Analysis* (Pacific Palisades, CA: Goodyear Publishing Co., 1969), pp. 240-254.

program to be doing, and the final impacts of the program.[19] Lack of uniformity among the procedures used by different local administrators to record data also undermines the accuracy and reliability of the information upon which the performance indicators are based.

The Work Incentive Program (WIN), established to help adults receiving Aid to Families with Dependent Children, serves as a useful example. Labor's Employment and Training Administration announces periodically WIN's achievements, as it did in the announcement of December 21, 1978 that the "WIN program placed 300,000 welfare recipients in jobs last year." The announcement went on to claim that "savings to the taxpayers amounted to well over double the cost of the WIN program." This pre-Christmas announcement must have been adequate cause to raise the Yuletide spirit of all readers. The trouble is that the "analysis" failed to call to the attention of the readers that welfare recipients have traditionally moved in and out of the AFDC program and that most of the 300,000 placed (assuming the statistics are correct) would have left the rolls in the absence of that support.

On the other hand, evaluating a program with inappropriate measures may condemn an effort that is achieving legitimate and desirable results. When the General Accounting Office (GAO) evaluated the Neighborhood Youth Corps, it concluded that the program was ineffective because it failed to reduce the school dropout rate for disadvantaged youth. However, the dropout rate is a function of far deeper social forces and systemic shortcomings that NYC could address alone.[20] The GAO evaluation almost certainly would have been more useful if it had examined the income transfer spillover effects of the youth program on poor families.

Early evaluations of the countercyclical public service jobs created under the Comprehensive Employment and Training Act

---

19. Robert S. Gay and Michael E. Borus, "Validating Performance Indicators for CETA," Employment and Training Administration, U.S. Department of Labor, 1978.

20. General Accounting Office, *Federal Manpower Training Programs—Conclusions and Observations* (Washington: General Accounting Office, 1977).

of 1973 harshly denounced the extent of "fiscal substitution." Evaluators stated that the net job creation effect of the public service job programs was minimal because local governments were laying off municipal employees one day and hiring them with federal manpower dollars the next. Subsequent studies, however, showed a different picture. Without the job creation funds, local governments would have been forced to lay off workers and cut municipal services.[21] While the simple before-after analysis of the impact of job creation measures showed a greatly diminished impact on local unemployment, the more sophisticated analysis accounting for *what would have happened* without the measures indicated two positive accomplishments: first, the programs were having a larger impact on total employment than had been previously suspected, and second, the job creation measures were proving to be very effective countercyclical revenue sharing tools. The latter is valuable on a more abstract level as well in that it recognized secondary impacts beyond the original design objectives of the programs that nonetheless proved to be important. In short, evaluations assessing the merits of the job measure strictly in terms of its stated objectives may be methodologically proper but are often misleading indicators of the accomplishments of the programs.

A very serious risk associated with the use of any indicator is that analysts may accept without questioning the story they are purported to tell. Even if indicators are valid, accurate, and reliable proxies for the variables that need to be examined, correlations do not necessarily imply causation because indicators also must have a finite number of components if they are to remain consistent and useful over time. However, the cost of that consistency is high where variables that are either hard to measure or only occasionally important have been omitted for the sake of administrative convenience or to save costs. The alternative of partial measurements is often justified on the grounds that they provide *some* enlightment. "The problem, of course, is that a little

---

21. Richard P. Nathan, Robert F. Cook, Janet M. Galchick, Richard W. Long, and Associates, "Preliminary Report: Monitoring the Public Service Employment Program" (Washington: The Brookings Institution, February 15, 1978).

bit of the truth is sometimes taken for the whole—and half-right analysis can be worse than none."[22]

EFFECTIVE COMPARED TO WHAT?

Even if useful indicators were easy to choose, and goals and objectives had been clearly established, a nagging question would remain: "What *would have* happened in the absence of the intervention complex?" Evaluation designs must fully assess "before" and "after" when measuring the net effects of social programs.

The biggest obstacle faced in this aspect of the evaluator's task is the difficulty of securing appropriate control groups. The overall objective is to gauge impact by comparing the performance of program completers to how well they would have fared in the absence of the program. Since it is impossible to measure both the effects of participation and nonparticipation on the same individual, evaluators try to find a group of persons similar to program participants in every way except with respect to program enrollment. The hope, then, is that any post-program differences observed between the control group and program participants can be attributed to the effects of program participation.

There are major impediments to obtaining appropriate control groups, though. The evaluators encounter their first challenges in finding enough persons with comparable characteristics, setting up the group, and keeping it intact. Evaluators studying a series of rural midwestern youth projects were unable to assemble a control group because, once the projects were implemented, there were too few nonparticipating Indians remaining for a satisfactory control group. Studies attempting to measure the effect that youth employment programs of the late 1960s had on school retention were plagued by an inability of the evaluators to assemble a control group comparable to the program participants with respect to important socioeconomic variables.

---

22. Walton J. Francis, "What Social Indicators Don't Indicate," *Evaluation,* Vol. 1, No. 2, 1973, p. 82.

Control group methodologies are most susceptible to the problems associated with comparability assumptions. A longitudinal study attempting to measure the duration of gains experienced by Job Corps participants, relied on "no-shows"—persons who were accepted for the Job Corps but failed to enroll at a center—as a substitute for a genuine control group. By doing so, evaluators undermined the impact of their conclusions with doubts as to whether the no-shows were comparable to participants, or instead, failed to participate in Job Corps because they did not need the Job Corps' services.[23] In another follow-up study that sought to measure earning gains of trainees in employment and training programs, the evaluator constructed a control group using records of persons from the general working population who were part of the Social Security Administration's continuous work history sample.[24] The validity of this approach was questioned because Social Security data do not capture critical differences between the general working population and persons from poverty populations participating in the training programs. Using the continuous work history sample as a control, all the evaluator could validly show was ". . . how the changes in the earnings of MDTA trainees compare with those of the average worker. Since most trainees come from disadvantaged backgrounds, it is unreasonable to expect their earnings to rise by as much as the average worker. . . ."[25]

There are also ethical problems associated with the use of control groups. The idea underlying their use is that they are equivalent in every way to the experimental groups *except* that they do not take part in the program being evaluated. The best way to assure equivalence is to randomly select members of both the control and experimental groups from the same population.

---

23. Sar A. Levitan and Benjamin Johnston, *The Job Corps: A Social Experiment That Works* (Baltimore: The Johns Hopkins University Press, 1975), p. 96.

24. David J. Farber, "Changes in the Duration of the Post Training Period in Relative Earnings Credits of Trainees," Manpower Administration, U.S. Department of Labor, August 1971.

25. Herman P. Miller, "Critique of David Farber's Method of Evaluating the Gains in Earnings of MDTA Trainees," prepared by the National Manpower Policy Task Force for the Manpower Administration, U.S. Department of Labor, September 1972.

Two ethical questions arise: Is it fair to exclude any person from participation in a program? Even if exclusion is justified because limited resources restrict the number of persons that can be served, is it just to select that person in a random, arbitrary fashion?

In medical research, when new drugs and medical procedures are being tested, the requirement for strict experimental conditions and control groups is commonly accepted. But in the early stages, where the potential risks are greatest, animals are used. Only when the obvious risks detectable in animals are first removed is the use of human control groups in a clinical setting generally accepted.[26] In contrast, use of control groups in social experimentation and program evaluation has not been able to require such a high degree of acceptance. People have to be used from the outset, when the unknowns are greatest, and often with no more justification than a hunch or political pressure to attempt any solution. Social experimentation is disadvantaged also because it cannot be carried out in a protected, clinical climate. Rather, it must operate in the public forum where it is open to public scrutiny and answerable for short-run as well as long-run effects. It also tends to be a controversial issue because it concentrates so heavily on the low-income, "disadvantaged" groups, and many observers are convinced that they have been dissected, analyzed, and studied enough.

Because of the ethical considerations, the use of control groups in social research has touched some very sensitive nerves in past social welfare undertakings. When guidelines were being developed for the evaluation of Elementary and Secondary Education Act Title I programs, the use of control groups was considered. The Office of Education decided against them to avoid "some deserving Title I kinds [being] denied services for the sake of experimentation. At the state level the feeling was that Title I was not a research program and therefore control groups were not to be used."[27] When researchers tried to select a random

---

26. John Mann, "Technical and Social Difficulties in the Conduct of Evaluative Research," in *Readings in Evaluation Research,* Francis Caro, editor (New York: Russell Sage Foundation, 1971), p. 181.

27. Wholey, *et al.,* p. 90.

control group in rural youth employment and training programs, they encountered resistance because the process of random selection was not acceptable to community leaders and school administrators.[28] The solution chosen was to draw the members of the control group from another jurisdiction that was not participating in the program.

SOCIAL EXPERIMENTATION: PANACEA OR PLACEBO?

Some critics argue that, considering all the time, effort, and resources invested in social initiatives in the last 15 years, the payoff in added knowledge and insights has been extremely limited. Causal relationships are as difficult as ever to document. There is still too much speculation and too little proof to distinguish between significant or inconsequential variables. There is a lack of coherence and consistency about the meaning, to say nothing of the lessons, that can be garnered from the data collected in connection with the vast social program experience of the 1960s and 1970s.

Systematic social experimentation is often held up as the Rosetta Stone that will make it possible to decipher the knowledge buried in voluminous, disparate and incomprehensible data. Alice Rivlin views systematic social experimentation as a policy tool in which "innovation should be tried in enough places to establish its capacity to make a difference and the conditions under which it works best."[29] Experimentation may also provide a mutually beneficial link between basic and "applied" (or evaluative) research. Advocates see experimental programs as contributing to the knowledge that analysts need to make substantive contributions to program evaluation and policy design.[30]

28. Joseph Reid and Guy Miles, "Final Report on an Evaluation of Three Experimental Rural Youth Projects: The Projects' First Year," North Star Research and Development Institute evaluation prepared for the Manpower Administration, U.S. Department of Labor, May 1974, p. 7.

29. Alice Rivlin, *Systematic Thinking for Social Action* (Washington: The Brookings Institution, 1971), p. 91.

30. Harold Orlans, *Contracting for Knowledge* (San Francisco: Jossey-Bass Publishers, 1973), pp. 111-126.

At first blush, systematic social experimentation appears to be an attractive solution to at least some evaluators, as well as to many social scientists. When it works, it can identify cause-effect relationships essential for sound program evaluation and development. But experimental strategies are costly and demand elaborate design and meticulous attention to detail. It is not clear at all that the returns justify the effort. Two sets of factors limit the final usefulness of social experimentation. First, the presumed experimental conditions that distinguish this strategy from less rigorous approaches are almost impossible to achieve. Second, even where they supposedly can be achieved, the simplistic notions about cause and effect that underlie experimentation strategies fail to capture either the full effect of program intervention or to satisfactorily document the influence of nonexperimental variables.

The New Jersey Graduated Work Incentive experiment illustrates many of the pitfalls that exist in experimental design. It was sponsored by the antipoverty agency, Office of Economic Opportunity, in 1967 to gain insights about the impacts of a guaranteed income program upon work behavior. Experimental and control groups were assembled in four cities to test the reactions of participants to different combinations of guaranteed income levels and marginal tax rates.

The experiment cost $8 million, of which about one-third went to actual cash payments for the participating families. The experiment itself ran four years and more than two additional years were taken up in planning and later analysis. The final report was published in July 1974. Based on the evidence collected in the experiment, the authors concluded that there was no significant pattern of decreased work effort associated with the guaranteed annual income program.[31]

The overhead of the New Jersey experiment is a useful starting point for an examination of the costs of systematic experimentation. Two-thirds of the total cost of the project were allocated for

---

31. David Kershaw and Jerilyn Fair, *The New Jersey Income-Maintenance Experiment* (New York: Academic Press, 1976).

study and evaluation. This included assembling the research staff, selecting the sample populations for the control and experimental groups, conducting interviews, terminating the experiment, and preparing the final report. The experiment proved more expensive to set up than anticipated because of the difficulty of getting an adequate racial balance in each experimental income-range sample. Thorough and controlled documentation required frequent interviews and reporting. Control group participants were interviewed quarterly and reported income monthly. Experimental group participants were interviewed monthly and reported income bi-weekly.

Nonetheless, obvious flaws could not be avoided. In fact, inherent in the very design, so carefully constructed, was an observation process that interfered with normal behavior. The experimenters did not analyze the ramifications of extensive observations, only noting the effects of observation insofar as it made the experimental group more adept at filling out the income forms than the control group because the former completed them more frequently.

Experimentation with the wrong variable is a potential flaw that can completely vitiate the experimental approach. The primary objective of the New Jersey experiment was to test how different minimum income levels and marginal tax rates affected the incentive of participants to work. The evidence showed no significant pattern of persons dropping out of the labor force in response to high support levels or high marginal tax rates. The experimenters concluded that a negative income tax plan would not cause people to deliberately cut back their income.[32] Yet later evidence indicated that, while the effects of incremental changes in support levels and marginal tax rates were not significant, those associated with the level of in-kind benefits appeared to be. These authors interpret the results of the experiment as suggesting that while increases or decreases in marginal tax rates might not induce

---

32. David Kershaw and Felicity Skidmore,"The New Jersey Graduated Work Incentive Program," prepared by Mathematica, Inc. for the Office of Economic Opportunity, July 1974.

persons to change their employment status, changes in their eligibility for medical benefits and housing aid probably would.[33]

The high costs of an experiment do not ensure conclusive results. Four years after the New Jersey experiment was completed, HEW and Labor unveiled the results of another guaranteed income experiment carried out at the other end of the continent. The Seattle, Washington and Denver, Colorado income maintenance experiments involving 4,800 families at a cost of $60 million conducted over a three-year period, found that income guarantees did reduce incentive to work and dependency. The investigators in this demonstration also noted that the guaranteed income increased divorce rates, a variable ignored in the earlier project.

The negative findings did not persuade or discourage true believers though. One analyst suggested that the measured decline in marital bliss "is an acceptable price one must pay for greater equality between men and women. . . ."[34] Another observer declared, "There is more to marriage than economics, after all."[35] More fundamental, a closer examination of the data disclosed the need to disaggregate the sample studied. Averages can be misleading, sometimes hiding more than they reveal. Some participants reduced or stopped working, but they used their time to gain an education leading to better jobs. Others worked fewer hours to take care of their children.[36]

Underlying this redefinition of issues is the dilemma that constantly faces evaluators and which assumes particular importance in an experiment: Which variable should be tested? Evaluators often go after data on race when they should be paying attention to sex, age, or education of program enrollees. Or they

---

33. Council of Economic Advisers, *Economic Report of the President* (Washington: Government Printing Office, 1976), p. 95.

34. Irwin Garfinkel cited in *Employment and Training Reporter,* November 22, 1978, p. 173.

35. Tom Joe cited in Linda E. Demkovich, "Good News and Bad News for Welfare Reform," *National Journal,* December 30, 1978, p. 2063.

36. Robert Reinhold, "Test in Seattle Challenges Minimum-Income Plan," *New York Times,* February 5, 1979.

may try to link low income and inadequate medical care to high infant mortality rates instead of more important environmental factors. Then, when the findings turn out to be unsatisfactory, evaluators can hide behind the refuge that the variables examined were irrelevant or should not be controlling policy formulation.

The Youth Incentive Entitlement Pilot Projects, mandated by the 1977 amendments to the Comprehensive Employment and Training Act, is another experiment whose high costs may fail to pay off in insights. This 30-month, $220 million search for cures to youth unemployment uses elaborate experimental designs to test the effect of a guaranteed job on school retention. Added sophistication may not make the answers any less elusive though. So far, the projects seem as wrong-headed in their premises as they are ambitious in their research objectives. Neither education nor employability and training experts have found much evidence that a lack of income is the only factor, or even the most important of many factors, contributing to the dropout problem. Even if it were, researchers are finding that the notion of a guaranteed job introduces a host of complications that may prevent evaluators from testing their central hypothesis.

Choosing the key variables is like shooting in the dark. Consequently, systematic experimentation may be inefficient. On a pilot basis (the only economically feasible way to use systematic experimentation), the number of beneficiaries is small compared to that in a full-scale program. If the experiment fails, losses are minimized. But if it succeeds, the time spent on the experiment (six years for the New Jersey experiment) is lost. And if national conditions change, the benefit of the successful experiment may never be realized. Harold Orlans describes the problem well: "Since the government's goals will and should change, as conditions dictate, the timing of research is as critical as its technical adequacy. A quick study yielding gross estimates can be more useful than a laborious study producing more information about a situation that no longer exists."[37]

---

37. Harold Orlans, "Making Social Research More Useful to Government," *Social Science Information,* December 1968, p. 153.

Another factor that diminishes the value of social experimentation is the incremental nature of gaining insights into social phenomena. Experience indicates that social knowledge does not make giant leaps forward. Even the best run social experiment is likely to show the way for making only marginal improvements. In light of this, the reluctance of program administrators to justify the expense of experimentation when less systematic approaches can yield almost the same insights and opportunity for improvement is understandable.[38]

Perhaps the most serious drawback to systematic social experimentation concerns the assumption that experimental conditions are attainable in a social setting. Three uncontrollable outside factors influenced the New Jersey experiment. The first outside influence was anticipated: participant and community attitude towards the experiment. There was reluctance to cooperate with "do gooders" studying the poor. Program designers were also concerned about participant reactions to the varying of benefits on a random basis, as well as community and control group acceptance of an experiment that excluded benefits altogether for the latter group. Inevitably, some militant community groups attacked the experiment, but their resistance collapsed when they became convinced that the choice was between half a loaf or none; while the experiment precluded giving money to the control group, the experimental group would have received no support in the absence of the trial program. The obstacles were overcome in that experiment, but the resistance to being guinea pigs is chronic and hard to overcome. It may be insurmountable when the benefits of participation are not clear.

A second serious disturbance in the New Jersey experiment was the January 1969 change in state law that qualified families headed by unemployed fathers to receive AFDC. This change, also beyond the control of the evaluators, altered an important experimental precondition. One of the reasons New Jersey was

---

38. John P. Gilbert, Richard Light, Frederick Mosteler, "Assessing Social Innovations: An Empirical Base for Benefit-Cost and Policy Analysis," *Benefit-Cost and Policy Analysis 1974: An Aldine Annual on Forecasting, Decisionmaking and Evaluation,* Richard Zeckhauser, editor (Chicago: Aldine Publishing Company, 1975).

originally selected as a site for testing the negative income tax was the lack of any competing welfare program for unemployed fathers (or plans for one). In order to minimize the competition and overlap between the two programs, the experimenters added another group of participants who received higher guaranteed support payments. This raised the costs of the experiment and necessitated payments in excess of the poverty guidelines.[39]

The political context of an experiment can destroy the illusion of a social laboratory. The New Jersey experiment encountered just this kind of problem with this external factor also. Although social experimentation is more akin to basic research than are other program evaluation techniques, it is still apt to be more topical than social scientists may wish when experimental niceties yield to political exigencies. Two observers of the New Jersey study noted that "it was inconceivable to everyone that political reality would overtake the experiment."[40] Yet, in August 1969, when the project had been underway barely a year, the Nixon Administration unveiled its Family Assistance Plan. Seeking to reform the welfare system, it included a negative income tax, among other features. Since the New Jersey experiment was the most prominent source of empirical data about the relationship between a negative income tax and work behavior, the project administrators were called to testify before the House Ways and Means Committee. At their first appearance, they responded to the congressional inquiries in general terms. Thereafter, they released their preliminary findings that supported the Family Assistance Plan in principle. The report opened the experiment to close scrutiny by the General Accounting Office and the Senate Finance Committee. The latter attempted to obtain confidential records of participating families—a potentially disastrous action from the experimenters' point of view. The disclosure issue died, but the project administrators were hard put to counteract the GAO criticisms. The experimenters learned a lesson and confined subsequent public comments to specific questions without taking sides in the debate.[41]

39. Kershaw and Skidmore, pp. 8-29.
40. *Ibid.*, p. 44.
41. *Ibid.*, p. 46.

After their encounter with the political perils in a researcher's life, the project officials noted that as experiments became more relevant to current political decisions, legislative inquiries were more likely to pose sensitive issues and threaten the success of an experiment. It became evident that, to be effective, social research requires high standards of scholarship *and* political skills, that it cannot be merely a mental exercise for academics in ivory towers. It is a process of inquiry that must be able to withstand the scrutiny of a curious and sometimes hostile public, not to mention the scrutiny of other scholars. The work of a social scientist demands sensitivity to the implications of the answers being sought and to the pressures that the policy arena exerts. Otherwise, as two observers commented in regard to the New Jersey experiment, serious complications may arise not merely from bad judgment, but even considerably more from plain bad luck.[42]

Bad luck, however, is not always solely a matter of random chance. While specific problems cannot always be predicted, general difficulties can usually be anticipated with a great deal of confidence. Any situation mixing evaluation/research with program administration is bound to run into difficulties, as local manpower administrators discovered in the 1960s when they tried to impose an evaluation design on the new programs. They rediscovered similar conflicts late in the 1970s in an attempt to accommodate the needs of evaluators assessing youth employment and training programs.[43]

The Labor Department's Neighborhood Youth Corps program, adapted to the needs of rural youth, offers additional insight into the pitfalls of the experimental approach. The Labor Department initially set up three experimental projects corresponding to three basic rural economies in northern Minnesota, southern Iowa, and central Nebraska. The design was later expanded to include an experimental subgroup of American Indians in Minnesota.

42. Peter H. Rossi and Katharine C. Lyall, "An Overview Evaluation of the NIT Experiment," in *Evaluation Studies Review Annual,* Vol. 3, Thomas D. Cook, editor (Beverly Hills, CA: Sage Publications, 1978), pp. 412-428.

43. John Walsh, Case Study appearing in *The Unfolding Youth Initiatives* (Washington: U.S. Department of Labor, 1978), pp. 76-66.

Unlike the New Jersey experiment, the rural youth project was to have a short observation period in the hope of getting a quick, conclusive verdict. As usual, events did not go exactly as planned. Selection of the experimental and control groups took longer than expected, and the addition of the Indian sample caused further delay. Funding delays held up the start of the project for 15 months. A summer program component was run on a makeshift basis in two states and omitted in the third. The school-year projects were delayed until Christmas. First year operations were beset by staffing and training problems, local suspicion, and a lack of cooperation. The lack of uniform compliance with federal guidelines required evaluators to deal with three distinct projects, reducing the comparability of findings. The initially ambitious experiment was transformed into a brief, fragmented project. Needless to say, the results of what was supposed to be a fairly definitive experiment were, at best, tentative.

There are some lessons for the evaluator to learn. It is difficult to achieve controlled conditions that are adequate to justify the choice of the experimental mode. Because the contractor could not come up with an American Indian control group, the usefulness of the final results for adapting the program to the unique needs of Indian youth was seriously limited. The lack of uniformity among the three projects made it difficult to generalize about which approach to youth employment was effective in which kind of economy. A variety of community, political, and social forces disrupted well-considered plans and reasonable timetables.[44]

In principle, an experiment may be the most precise way to measure the effectiveness of a social program, but in practice it is difficult to implement. It is time-consuming and can inhibit timely, innovative solutions. Ideally, eliminating ineffective solutions may save money. But, when inherent delays postpone the implementation of effective measures, the result is social waste. The desire of decisionmakers to make careful, well-documented decisions based on fact is commendable, but considering the costs in time and lost opportunity, policymakers may have to

---

44. Reid and Miles, *op. cit.*

settle instead for intuition, normative judgments, and experience. Social problems are too complex, their patterns too elusive, and the need for action too pressing. Frequently, as welfare reformers reconfirmed in 1978, pretensions of scientific rigidity and the advocacy of experimentation may be pretexts for avoiding action or substituting less costly programs.

MAKING USE OF EVALUATION FINDINGS

The methodological challenge of evaluating social programs is only half the battle facing practitioners. The other half is the struggle to get evaluation findings into policymaking channels. There are two obstacles to be overcome: the mechanical process of managing disparate evaluation findings and the process of generalizing some lessons from those findings.

Managing Information

The history of information management services goes back to the libraries of classical times and the early encyclopedias. Modern systems were developed in medical sciences, but only more recently have the social sciences been given the same kind of treatment. The government's attempts to keep track of its social program evaluation intelligence have yet to be developed beyond the primitive stage. The Institute of Scientific Information prepares the *Social Science Citation Index*. It offers literature in practically all social science research as well as social program evaluation. A more recent attempt to keep track of what has been done in the field of social program evaluation has also taken place outside the federal establishment: Databank of Program Evaluation (making for the unfortunate acronym DOPE), established in 1972 at the UCLA School of Public Health to accumulate and analyze evaluations of programs in the mental health and social action fields. The service identifies programs that have been evaluated, provides a summary of the program, describes how the evaluation was performed, and the findings. The DOPE data bank is assembled from material published in journals, contacts with selected experts, and a search of already existing data banks.[45]

Inside the government, indexing and referencing services whose functions are to keep tabs on social science research findings and, in particular, social program evaluation findings, have been slower to catch on. This has not, however, been due to a lack of attention to the need for information management.

HEW has initiated a number of systems to keep track of progress in the evaluation area. The Evaluation Documentation Center follows evaluations at all stages of progress. Its purpose is to prevent duplication in the evaluation planning process and to serve as a reference service for outsiders trying to track down experts. HEW also operates Project Share, a technical assistance information retrieval and dissemination system oriented toward serving the information needs of HEW program administrators in state and local governments. It was established primarily to keep track of information bearing on program operation and program management, and offers very little intelligence about the impact or effectiveness of HEW programs. At HEW's bureau level, only the Office of Education has attempted an elaborate information management system: the Education Resources Information Clearinghouse (ERIC), a comprehensive data bank of evaluative research and other education literature. ERIC's most serious weakness is that it contains an overabundance of detail, which often makes it too cumbersome to be useful.

The Department of Labor has a lesser information management problem than HEW. The department is smaller and narrower in scope, and the bulk of its evaluation work has focused on employment and training efforts. There, the need for a formal system for keeping tabs on the state of the research art and the information it yields has not been acute.

---

45. Daniel M. Wilner, *et al.,* "Databank of Program Evaluations," *Evaluation,* Vol. 1, No. 3, 1973, and Robert W. Hetherington, *et al.,* "The Nature of Program Evaluation in Mental Health," *Evaluation,* Vol. 2, No. 1, 1974.

Evaluation: For Investment or Consumption?

The lack of a clear distinction between evaluation and research is easily discernible. The federal government's Office of Management and Budget (OMB), marked by a predilection for neat compartmentalization, has decreed that the distinction between the two activities lies in the different roles they play in the decisionmaking process. Consequently, all agencies engaged in both evaluation and research must make administrative distinctions between the two, although they are hard put to spell out the differences.

In line with the distinction with little difference, OMB adopts a fairly narrow concept of program evaluation as "a systematic process of management which seeks to analyze federal programs (or their components) to determine the manner in and extent to which they have achieved (or are achieving) their objectives." OMB generally views evaluation as confined to existing programs, although some elements of policy analysis, specifically those concerned with the estimation of the impact of program options, fall under a broader definition.[46] Within this rather confining definition, the agency places great emphasis upon the "decision relevance" of evaluations and the desirability of making evaluations that contribute clearly to decisions. In other words, evaluation findings should be applicable primarily to program-related decisions about operations, funding levels, and policy directions.

In the program agencies, though, evaluation is perceived as serving somewhat broader objectives. Evaluation managers are happy to point out the relevance and effects of their findings on policy choices and other program decisions. But they also murmur under their collective breaths that the search for a one-to-one correspondence between evaluation findings and decisions based upon these findings is not an appropriate indicator of how effective evaluations are, and that any attempt to force evaluation

---

46. U.S. Office of Management and Budget, "Problems in Evaluation Design: A Background Paper," October 1976, pp. 2-3, and "Evaluation Management: A Background Paper," May 1975.

management into a dressed-up "management information system" would be a mistake. In contrast to the OMB view of evaluation as a process tailored to serve specific needs, the managers of program evaluations in the executive branch see it more as a learning exercise. They hope that through an inductive process of successive reviews, larger patterns will emerge; that evaluation findings will form a patchwork of new lessons to be knitted together so as to contribute to larger, generalized notions of social theory.[47] As part of that larger "body of knowledge," evaluative findings build on the existing evidence to advance social theory.

However, the claim that evaluation and research activities are contributing cumulatively to the aggregation of knowledge remains an assertion. Given only skimpy evidence that evaluation produces immediate impacts, evaluators are forced to lay claim to long-run achievements. It might be more accurate to say that the immediate contributions of evaluations are marginal and their long-run cumulative impact remains to be determined.

BUILDING A USEABLE BASE

A National Research Council report has criticized the research and development program of the Department of Labor's Employment and Training Administration for not establishing a base of knowledge upon which future research can build. Recognizing that knowledge building in a relatively new field is bound to be uneven, it noted that "expanding and cumulative effects cannot be obtained unless successive analyses of a problem build consciously on earlier results."[48] To Allen Schick, the problem represented a failure to integrate evaluation findings and policymaking. "There often is little follow-up to an evaluation; once done, the case is closed and the evaluators move on to other

---

47. Johan Galtung, *Theory and Methods of Social Research* (New York: Columbia University Press, 1969), pp. 9-36.
48. *Knowledge and Policy in Manpower* (Washington: National Academy of Sciences, 1975), p. 26.

matters. Each evaluation is regarded as a discrete special event rather than as part of an overall policy process."[49]

In both instances, the underlying assumption is that evaluators, like brickmasons, can lay a foundation and then build on it. However, there is little evidence for such a claim. Merely drawing parallels to experiences in the physical or life sciences does not provide convincing proof that evaluation and research can be developed into coherent parts of a systematized body of knowledge for use in social policy. The "softness" and unpredictability of social science phenomena contribute to this difficulty by making learning, if it can be achieved at all, a slow, tedious process. The mistaken assumption is that if a "critical mass" of knowledge is gathered, progress will necessarily follow. An airplane builder gets off the ground only after establishing a base of understanding in mechanical engineering, aerodynamics, basic physics, and materials properties. Knowledge does not start accumulating until there is a base of theory and evidence in all the component areas and the prototype airplane has successfully gotten off the ground. The knowledge building goes on from the original base and from what is learned in that first uncertain flight.

Research in the life sciences shares the same problems and hopes in pursuit of the accumulation of knowledge. In the early 1960s, the Office of Science and Technology established a study group to review research management policies and to recommend steps for improving the return on research investments. One of the group's findings was that a body of knowledge could not be started and built in discrete blocks of knowledge or in discrete fields of study. Because of a high degree of interdependence among areas of research, the group noted, more meaningful conclusions rested upon a synthesis of knowledge from more than one area. The group concluded that before research could have any kind of

49. Allen Schick, "Evaluating Evaluation: A Congressional Perspective," *Legislative Oversight and Program Evaluation,* Proceedings of a Seminar sponsored by the Congressional Research Service for the U.S. Senate Committee on Government Operations (Washington: Government Printing Office, May 1976), pp. 352-353.

expanding and cumulative effect, there had to be an undifferentiated mass of knowledge, a relatively unstructured body of experience. From this base, it was asserted, a paradigm could be fashioned and learning could go on, drawing from many sources as needed and building upon what had already been discovered.[50]

Whatever merits this learning process may have for the physical and biological sciences, the approach is not promising for the evaluation of social programs. The difficulty is that similar conditions cannot be replicated in the evaluation of social programs. Mechanical engineering principles and basic physics are equally as applicable today as in the days of Faraday. Newton and Einstein both lived with the same law of gravity. Social institutions change, however, and evaluations of yesteryear remain only of historical interest to today's evaluators.

However, that does not mean that evaluation and research activities can go off undirected or with only passing attention to how findings can be incorporated into a generalized body of knowledge. Still, there is little reason to hope that there is much gold to be mined in old findings. Agency evaluation and research managers readily admit that they pay inadequate attention to the manner in which new efforts add to what is already known. The reason for this neglect may be the fact that the payoff is negligible.

INSTITUTIONAL ARRANGEMENTS

The changing evaluation literature has focused either on substance of findings or methodological issues. But with only a few exceptions, there has been little attention given to the practitioners of the trade, and virtually no consideration given to the influences that institutions wield in determining the purposes of evaluations or the uses to which they are put.

The fact that evaluators have tended to pay little attention to the arguments of their trade is not necessarily due to excessive

---

50. *Biomedical Science and Its Administration: A Study of the National Institutes of Health* (Washington: Government Printing Office, 1965).

modesty. It is more reasonable to assume that the neglect is due to methodological factors. Institutional influences on evaluation are hard to describe and impossible to capture in quantitative terms. Selecting the variables to study, collecting data on them, and interpreting the data all involve an enormous amount of subjectivity. Under those conditions, even the illusion of objectivity is hard to achieve. Any attempt to tackle the institutional issues invites attacks (as the present authors can testify) on methodological grounds and almost certainly will be disputed as a misinterpretation of findings—a safe accusation since any interpretation is arbitrary. These conditions reduce substantially the incentives for examining the institutional issues.

But the more practical aspects accounting for the neglect of the institutional aspects relating to evaluation also cannot be ignored. Evaluators are no more prone to bite the hands that feed them than any other group of persons concerned about their own well being. Since governmental agencies account for most of the support for evaluation, there is no pecuniary return to most of the practitioners for doing critical evaluations of their supporters. Existing discussions of evaluation supporters tend to be, therefore, public relations jobs, although exceptions occur. It takes a courageous administrator of evaluation programs to subject an agency to critical evaluation. An exception that can be found in the literature is an evaluation of the Office of Research and Development in the Department of Labor.[51]

Institutional factors, whether or not they are recognized, have a pervasive influence on the federal government's social program evaluation policies. The purpose that evaluation serves, the way it is done, and the manner in which evaluation findings are incorporated into policy are directly affected by these forces.

A useful starting point for an analysis of institutional factors associated with evaluation is the constitutional roles that differentiate the legislative and executive branches. In the most formal terms, the legislative branch establishes policies and the

---

51. *Knowledge and Policy in Manpower, op. cit.*

executive branch bears responsibility for implementing them. This constitutional basis does not force a clear differentiation between evaluations in the two branches. Indeed, in a case-by-case analysis, there are probably more similarities than there are differences in the way evaluation is undertaken and the findings used.

The constitutionally differentiated roles, however, do establish an underlying mode for checks and balances. There is an inevitable tension between the two branches, and evaluation is used as a weapon in the adversary relationship.

3
Evaluation in the
Legislative Branch

Evaluation takes on a number of forms in the legislative branch. Congressional committees do it all the time. Their work ranges from gumshoe assessments laden with anecdotal information to more careful and systematic reviews. The General Accounting Office does painstaking reviews of programs while the Congressional Research Service recycles evaluation literature prepared by the executive branch and others to produce a synthesis of current views. The binding force among all the legislative branch's evaluation work is its constitutional and institutional oversight role. The legislative branch has the duty to keep tabs on how the executive branch is carrying out congressional mandates. But although it gives legitimacy to the congressional evaluation role, the constitutional basis does not necessarily guarantee the effectiveness of these efforts. The purpose of this section is to examine how effectively Congress discharges those evaluation responsibilities.

CONGRESSIONAL OVERSIGHT

Congressional oversight is nebulous but all encompassing. One study of oversight activity lists no fewer than nine distinct definitions. They range from the narrow "review after the fact" to broad reviews of "almost everything members [of Congress] do, e.g., legislating, gathering information, campaigning, etc."[1]

1. Harrison W. Fox, Jr., "Oversight: Is Congress Doing Its Job?" Paper presented at the 1974 Annual Meeting of the American Political Science Association, pp. 6-7.

Regardless of the definition chosen, program evaluation is clearly a legitimate and important part of congressional oversight. In 1951, a member of Congress put it well, saying "I know of no means whereby Congress can assert its authority over national policies except through the expansion and improvement of investigative powers."[2] His sentiments were echoed a generation later by another congressman in a world that was, as far as federal social programs were concerned, light years removed from the simpler days of post-World War II America: "The oversight or evaluation function will allow Congress to begin to restore the balance of power between the executive branch and the legislative branch."[3]

Clearly, oversight is an integral part of congressional activity. And the more legislation Congress passes, the more activities there are to oversee and the more results there are to assess. A report on the operations of the senate cited three reasons for improving the capability of the Senate (and Congress) to stay on top of issues: the expansion of the powers of the presidency that was occurring at the expense of the legislative branch; the increasing complexity of legislative issues; and the explosive growth of knowledge and information.[4] That report, completed at the end of 1976, is one in a long list of commentaries coming from inside and outside the Congress calling for more and better congressional oversight—and evaluation. Whatever response emerges will be another addition to a growing list of measures taken to strengthen the oversight and evaluation capabilities of the legislative branch during the last several decades. The Legislative Reorganization Act of 1946 made specific reference to congressional oversight mandating standing committees to ". . . exercise continuous watchfulness of the execution by the administrative agencies. . . ."[5] The Legislative Reorganization Act of 1970 added specific provisions for

---

2. George Meader, "Congressional Investigations: Importance of the Fact-Finding Process," *University of Chicago Law Review,* Spring 1951, p. 450.

3. James J. Blanchard, *Zero-Base Budget Legislation,* in U.S. Congress, House Committee on the Budget (Washington: Government Printing Office, 1976), pp. 2-3.

4. *Toward a Modern Senate,* U.S. Congress, Final Report of the Commission on the Operation of the Senate (Washington: Government Printing Office, 1976), pp. 42-43.

5. Public Law 79-601, Section 136.

obtaining agency budget and performance data.[6] The Congressional Budget and Impoundment Control Act of 1974 extended the authority of congressional committees to carry out oversight and evaluation activities and laid new mandates on the congressional support agencies.[7]

The much debated "sunset" provisions, calling for the automatic termination of programs unless congressional oversight demonstrates that they are attaining their goals, offer another approach. Their justification was summed up by a congressional proponent: ". . . it is clear that we need a procedure that will require careful scrutiny of every spending program to determine whether it is operating effectively or needs modification or elimination."[8]

However much Congress does about evaluation and oversight is surely not done in ignorance of the need for oversight. Evaluation and oversight have been given a great deal of lip service and are, in principle, virtues of universal appeal. But in a body given to as much rhetoric as the U.S. Congress, all pronouncements must be taken with the proverbial grain of salt.

Congress obviously plays a leading role in shaping social policy. That has been the case in the last decade and a half especially, and it promises to be the case for the future, whether in an era of social program expansion or retrenchment. Granted, decisionmaking and policymaking will go on with or without oversight and evaluation procedures. But the quality of that policy formulation will hinge, to no small extent, upon the quality of oversight and evaluation activities supporting it. In short, the technical state of the art and the institutional arrangements for evaluation are crucial to the course of social policy.

There are identifiable kinds of oversight that correspond to each of four congressional decisionmaking mechanisms: legislative,

---

6. Public Law 91-510, Titles II and III.

7. Public Law 93-344.

8. Joseph R. Biden, Jr., *Government Economy and Spending Reform Act,* in U.S. Congress, Senate Government Operations Committee (Washington: Government Printing Office, 1976), p. 13.

fiscal and analytical, investigative, and authoritative. Each type of congressional-based oversight can be incorporated into the corresponding decisionmaking structure. Legislative oversight includes hearings, meetings, and reporting requirements. Through fiscal and analytical oversight—the power of the purse—the appropriations committees, joined more recently by the budget committees, determine the level of funding for given activities. Investigative oversight is carried out to control and discipline particular executive operations. Authoritative oversight operates through the periodic review and amendment of authorizing legislation and the confirmation of presidential appointees. Impeachment is perhaps the ultimate oversight.[9]

Evaluation as Part of Oversight

Program evaluation is particularly useful for legislative and fiscal oversight, shedding light on the effectiveness of alternative strategies or the effects of different funding levels on service delivery. But the quality and usefulness of evaluations are influenced not only by their methodology, but also by who is doing them.

As large as the legislative branch is—535 members of Congress and over 18,000 staff in 1978—it does not function as a single hierarchy as do the many bureaucracies in the executive branch. Instead there are 535 different decisionmakers, each, theoretically, with the same power and each with an independent power base and distinctive constituencies. In practice, of course, some members are more equal than others and the differences are embodied in the congressional pecking order. But the process of decisionmaking is less clear than in a hierarchical structure, information needs are much more fragmented and diverse, and political partisanship is a powerful motivating force.

Because of the large volume and complexity of the issues that come up for congressional consideration, there is an inescapable need for specialization and a division of labor. Most of the basic

---

9. Ward Sinclair, "The Man Who Perfected Oversight," *The Washington Post,* January 14, 1979, p. G-3.

substantive work on legislation is done in committees and subcommittees. And although any member of Congress can speak before the full House or Senate, there is no guarantee that anyone will listen. The principal forum for congressional and public influence that is brought to bear on an issue is the committee or subcommittee. That is where specialization takes root and where critical legislative powers lodge.

Evaluation by Congressional Committees

Formal congressional evaluations of social programs are customarily done by one of the support agencies, but the work of the committees should not be glossed over. Like Moliere's hero who spoke prose all his life and did not know it, congressional committees are continuously engaged in evaluation either as part of the regular authorization and appropriation process or as a distinct monitoring exercise. They lay out the important legislative issues and identify the crucial questions, providing specific guidance and instruction to the support agencies embarking on particular evaluation projects. The committees, in effect, act as the hub for congressional oversight and evaluation work.

Evaluation has long been recognized as a legitimate and significant committee function. However, committees rarely indulge in detailed reviews. Usually, they tend to rely on the support agencies to grind out program assessments, but there are notable exceptions.

The Joint Economic Committee's review of alternative income maintenance strategies, in which basic research was combined with evaluation, is an illustration of committee oversight at its best. The study was initiated after President Nixon introduced his Family Assistance Plan (FAP) in 1969. When the House Ways and Means Committee deliberations on FAP in 1970 and 1971 produced more questions than answers, committee member Congresswoman Martha Griffiths became convinced that federal income support activities deserved thorough scrutiny. She used her position as chair of the Joint Economic Committee's Fiscal Policy Subcommittee to get the job done. The final product, *Studies in*

Public Welfare, was three and a half years in the making. In addition to the 24 published staff studies, the output included four volumes of hearings, a summary report with recommendations approved by the subcommittee, and a draft bill advocating reform of public assistance.[10]

Studies in Public Welfare was an important addition to the burgeoning social welfare literature. Although the several monographs display a clear bias in favor of a guaranteed income scheme and strong opposition to in-kind aid programs, the total effort is a well-documented review of income support programs and a thorough analysis of the important issues in welfare policy. It spurred a more sophisticated level of debate and has had considerable influence in other respects. Its ultimate effect is uncertain, however. By spelling out in gruesome detail the pitfalls of alternative income maintenance strategies, the studies may have had the effect of squelching any initiatives. With the options and corresponding costs laid out, different sides could see without further debate the problems they were up against. While inherent in any solution, the discovery of these problems was instrumental in killing enthusiasm for a major overhaul of the welfare system at that time. That net effect may have been for the good, although in a perverse way, considering the intent of Congresswoman Griffiths and her staff director, Alair Townsend, to champion a guaranteed income support program. Part of the stimulus for *Studies in Public Welfare* was the projection for continued exponential growth in the AFDC caseload as occurred in the late 1960s; an erroneous assumption that failed to consider the fact that the system had already absorbed most of the potentially eligible population, and which ultimately tainted the entire study. In actuality any reform legislation based on the JEC Subcommittee's conclusions would have placed much of its focus on an illusory problem.

---

10. Alair Townsend, "Congressional Committee Case Studies: Studies in Public Welfare," in *Legislative Oversight and Program Evaluation,* U.S. Congress, Senate Committee on Government Operations (Washington: Government Printing Office, May 1976), pp. 206-218.

The Senate Banking, Housing and Urban Affairs Committee evaluation of existing and proposed housing legislation of 1973 serves as another illustration of detailed congressional oversight. It combined a dose of politics with proposals for new legislation. The evaluation consisted of several elements. First, the committee held oversight hearings following the President's imposition of a moratorium on new subsidized housing commitments under existing legislation. That was followed by hearings on a broad range of legislation introduced to improve housing in urban development programs, including an assessment of the housing and community development legislation proposed by the President. The final action was an analysis of the administration's position. The output of the evaluation effort was more than 3,000 pages of testimony, a report, and a bill that was eventually incorporated into the Housing and Community Development Act of 1974.

In both cases, the congressional subcommittees relied heavily upon outside help. Much of the background work for *Studies in Public Welfare* was done by executive agencies, the Congressional Research Service, the General Accounting Office and nongovernmental experts working either without compensation or without contract.[11] The review of housing programs, although a more modest project covering a shorter period of time, relied heavily on support provided by the Congressional Research Service.[12] Although both committees were in central positions to direct the evaluation work, neither could have done its evaluations relying on committee staff alone.

These two cases are the exception, however, not the rule. Congressional committees are not geared to conduct sustained evaluations, and the endorsement of evaluation in the Congressional Budget and Impoundment Control Act of 1974 is not likely to alter the situation. Since enactment, few consultants or contractors have been picked up by committees to do evaluation. The inclination appears to be to let the Congressional Research

11. *Ibid.*, p. 213.

12. *Critique of "Housing in the Seventies,"* U.S. Congress, Senate Committee on Banking, Housing and Urban Affairs (Washington: Government Printing Office, 1974).

Service, the General Accounting Office, and executive agencies do the evaluations and then use the products as the basis for further committee deliberations and action.

Limits on Committee Evaluation

The dearth of direct evaluation by congressional committees does not indicate a lack of interest on the part of Congress but, rather, reflects priorities, practicalities, and political realism. Because support agencies can do evaluation for them, committees place a low priority on direct monitoring or evaluation. It is a matter of using limited resources where they will do the most good. A second, related reason is the constraint imposed by limited staff expertise. Given the broad domain of some committees, their small staffs, the informal obligations of staff to the senior members, and the marginal interests of some in committee work, it is impossible to obtain high quality coverage in all areas. Moreover, the propensity of outside experts to offer advice is well known. Most experts are available on call and are only too eager to appear before congressional committees to share their wisdom without compensation. Thus, the premium staff skill is not the ability to evaluate programs and to offer solutions, but to raise the right questions.

The committees with jurisdiction over social programs have rarely utilized consultants for evaluation purposes. They prefer to let the Congressional Research Service, the General Accounting Office, or the Congressional Budget Office do the contracting, since committees are subject to inevitable political pressures to hire persons on the basis of *who* rather than *what* they know.

The experience of the House Agriculture Committee's effort to evaluate pending food stamp legislation taught that lesson well. In 1974, the U.S. Department of Agriculture contracted with Mathematica, a reputable research firm specializing in social legislation, to test the impact of changes in food stamp eligibility cutoffs and benefit levels on program clients. The first results of this analysis became available in late 1974. In mid-1975, shortly after the administration proposed food stamp reform legislation, the consulting firm examined the probable effects of the proposed legislation and found them to be less positive than promised by the sponsors of the legislation. The House Agriculture Committee then attempted to contract with the same firm to test for variables not considered by the Department of Agriculture. Political pressure doomed the project when the contractor was caught in a crossfire. The contractor's connection with the administration position made the organization suspect to some Democratic members, while conservatives were suspicious of the firm for an alleged liberal bias. The Agriculture Committee terminated the contract with Mathematica and relied instead on assistance from the Congressional Budget Office to assess the administration proposals and alternative approaches.

There are other compelling reasons why committees do not do their own evaluations. Partisan pressures are inevitable. An in-depth congressional study concluded: "At some early point advocacy tends to take over from objective inquiry. Delineation of the problem, acquisition of related knowledge, discovery of interested parties, committee markup, and floor consideration follow one upon another."[13]

The seniority system and procedures for assigning members to committees are also inhibiting factors. The success of *Studies in Public Welfare* can be largely attributed to the interest and substantive knowledge that Congresswoman Griffiths brought to bear on the staff's work. But her being in the right place at the right time was a product of chance, not planning. Seniority does not necessarily go hand-in-hand with substantive expertise. Congress lacks the institutional mechanism necessary to systematically tap that kind of interest, ability, and expertise necessary for program evaluation. *Studies in Public Welfare* was the product of a rare juxtaposition of executive initiative, congressional interest, and fortuitous committee assignments. The study probably would never have been undertaken if President Nixon had not proposed his Family Assistance Plan. Nor would the product have been as significant if the subcommittee had not

---

13. *Toward a Modern Senate,* p. 42.

secured an outstanding staff director with excellent connections in the welfare research community that stood ready to assist Congresswoman Griffiths in the exercise.

Congressional committees may find social program evaluation risky; it is frequently considered a no-win activity. It involves basic questions about the limits of individual responsibility and the obligation of society to care for those who cannot or do not take care of themselves. Consensus is hard to come by, emotions often get the upper hand, and subjective judgments must be accepted in formulating methodologies. The choice of methodologies and simplifying assumptions, as well as variables and hypotheses to be tested, are all open to debate. The kind of bickering the House Agriculture Committee encountered in its halting steps towards evaluating changes in food stamp legislation is more typical of congressional committee experience with social program evaluation than the experience of the Joint Economic Committee. Furthermore, the latter had no legislative authority, which might mean that the other members left the conduct of the studies and the drawing of the conclusions to the chair, aware that it would not directly affect legislation. In short, program evaluation is best left to nonpartisan congressional agencies that lack the authority to compete with legislative committees in sponsoring legislation.

The reluctance of congressional committees to get involved in evaluations is understandable. But assigning the responsibility to the support agencies has inherent shortcomings. The most crucial advantage of direct committee control is the assurance that the evaluation will be relevant to policy choices being made by Congress. In discussing the need for control in directing research efforts, the staff director responsible for producing *Studies in Public Welfare* cited the value of a strong committee staff ". . . not to control the *findings,* but to retain the desired *focus.*"[14] If evaluations are not kept on the targets Congress sets, and if they do not produce findings that can be applied during congressional decisionmaking, their net contribution may be marginal at best.

---

14. Townsend, p. 213.

THE CONGRESSIONAL BUDGET OFFICE

The Congressional Budget Office (CBO) is a relatively recent addition to the legislative scene. It was established under the provisions of the Congressional Budget and Impoundment Control Act of 1974 to help the House and Senate Budget Committees prepare the congressional budget and to provide technical assistance to other committees on budget matters in particular and on economic matters in general.[15] The idea was to create a congressional, nonpartisan think tank, supplemented by legislative committees within the traditional structure, which would be capable of providing nonpartisan analysis of the issues having an impact on the federal budget.

The initial CBO director, in describing the office's role, emphasized the constraints bearing down on its operations:

> CBO won't have the kind of depth to do program evaluation, where we actually get in and collect original information on programs. We will try to help as much as we can, but can't take over and we don't want to take over the functions of the General Accounting Office, which does not only the auditing of programs, but deals with evaluative work.[16]

So far, the Congressional Budget Office has relied in its evaluation work exclusively on data already available from executive agencies, the General Accounting Office, or private sources. The bulk of its work has centered on broad-based policy analyses and comparisons of the relative effectiveness of alternative social strategies. For example, in studying youth unemployment problems, CBO delineated the nature and extent of teenage unemployment and laid out some options for dealing with the problems.[17] But the paper did not address the specific

---

15. Public Law 93-344, Section 202.

16. Interview with Congressional Budget Office Director Alice Rivlin, *Congressional Quarterly Weekly Report,* September 6, 1975, p. 1925.

17. *Youth Unemployment: The Outlook and Some Policy Strategies,* U.S. Congress, Congressional Budget Office (Washington: Government Printing Office, 1978).

feasibility of the options or break any new ground in evaluating the effectiveness of past strategies. Another study compared the relative impact of job creation and training strategies. Again relying on evaluations of specific programs, the CBO laid out the policy options and the budget implications of each major effort.[18] In both, CBO integrated information obtained from past evaluations and other data to present policy alternatives.

Some members of Congress have criticized CBO's restraint in program evaluation. One leading advocate of budget reform and the new budget process claimed that his support of a relatively large staff for the Congressional Budget Office was based on the anticipation that CBO would carry on extensive program evaluation activities. His complaint was common, saying that Congress had "never been staffed up adequately to really challenge the testimony of executive department witnesses. We have no way of going behind the scenes and seeing whether they're using the funds we've given them wisely and whether their requests for additional funds are justified."[19]

There are some obvious differences of opinion over just what the appropriate role of the Congressional Budget Office should be in evaluating federal activities. At the same time, there has been some confusion about the role of the other congressional support agencies. Both program evaluation and certain aspects of policy analysis are conducted by the General Accounting Office and the Congressional Research Service. Against that backdrop, the attempt to get the Congressional Budget Office involved in these activities might suggest that these agencies are falling down in their responsibilities, and that CBO should fill the void. Given the newness of the office and the expanding capability of the Congressional Research Service and the General Accounting Office, it would be folly to speculate about the precise turf that CBO will stake out for itself. Clearly, there is a strong demand for independent, substantive, congressional evaluations of federal

---

18. *Public Employment and Training Assistance: Alternative Federal Approaches,* U.S. Congress, Congressional Budget Office (Washington: Government Printing Office, 1977).

19. Senator Henry Bellmon, *Congressional Quarterly Weekly Report,* September 6, 1975, pp. 1927-28.

programs with a minimum of reliance on executive help, and CBO as well as the two budget committees is playing a part in meeting that demand.

THE GENERAL ACCOUNTING OFFICE

A Changing Mission

The Budget and Accounting Act of 1921 established the General Accounting Office and the Bureau of the Budget. The Act carved the GAO role out of the Office of the Comptroller of the Treasury whose responsibility was to audit all executive branch operations, making the GAO an independent agency reporting to the Congress. The GAO was given the narrow responsibility of auditing as well as authorization to review program administration and operation, while the Bureau of the Budget was given much broader scope to handle budget and financial management affairs for the executive branch.

Until 1946, virtually all of GAO's activities involved financial auditing, with no formal oversight responsibilities and no substantive program assessment. Although the original GAO charter was sufficiently vague to authorize a wide range of activities, all of its work focused on keeping government officials honest by reviewing vouchers and assuring that money was spent properly. In fact, much of the value attributed to GAO's role was due not to its audit disclosures, but to the threat that the financial transactions of agencies would be scrutinized.[20]

The Legislative Reorganization Act of 1946 and the Government Corporation Control Act of 1945 expanded the narrow GAO view of what constituted good government. The two acts reflected the growing feeling that good government required more than keeping civil servants' hands out of the till. The reorganization act delineated an oversight role for Congress and broadened GAO's mission to support congressional oversight. Besides reviewing expenditures to check whether federal funds were spent honestly,

---

20. *The GAO Review,* Summer 1971, p. 25.

the law charged GAO with the responsibility to monitor appropriations to see whether they were being administered efficiently. The 1945 act broadened GAO's mandate, calling for more than checks on fiscal accountability. It set in motion a progression toward a broader definition of accountability to include management and program accountability.

But institutions change slowly. The broader responsibilities assigned by Congress notwithstanding, GAO continued for the next two decades to confine its work largely to financial and management audits. The surge of Great Society programs during the 1960s generated the need to put GAO into the role of social program evaluator. These controversial and multi-faceted programs demanded more substantive evaluation and, in some cases, established an explicit requirement for it. If a single event indicates the expansion of GAO evaluation responsibilities, the 1967 amendments to the Economic Opportunity Act requiring GAO to evaluate the antipoverty programs might be the proper mark. Either because the agency lacked confidence in its own capability to undertake this pioneer investigation, or because it sought to broaden the scope of its investigation, the GAO relied on contractors for guidance and assistance. But the final product, the *Review of Economic Opportunity Programs,* presented to Congress in 1969, was the first comprehensive evaluation of a social program done by GAO.

Reflecting this expansion in responsibilities, the GAO staff capability also changed over the years. Before 1946, the bulk of the agency's activities consisted of routine work determining whether or not expenditures were allowable and matching expenditures to supporting documentation. The work was done mostly by a technical staff of bookkeepers under the supervision of accountants and attorneys.

In 1946, when GAO's explicit mandate changed, Congress made new demands on the staff. Besides checking whether expenditures were authorized and documented, GAO had to audit accounts and programs to assure that government funds were used economically and efficiently. To carry out its responsibilities, GAO had to bolster its staff capabilities for comprehensive audits by employing more accountants. By the mid-1960s, (before the shift to more substantive program evaluation) auditors had come to comprise, along with accountants, roughly 90 percent of the professional staff.

The laws charging GAO with the responsibility to evaluate federal programs also drastically affected the bureaucratic structure of the agency during the 1960s. When GAO was set up in 1921, six operational divisions were transferred from the Treasury Department, each corresponding to an executive branch agency: the Treasury, the War Departments, the Navy, Interior, the Post Office, and the remaining departments. As the executive branch grew, GAO's primary audit work continued to be done along agency lines.

Administrative Structure

Compared to its first 45 years, the following decade of GAO's history was turbulent. Congress made major changes in GAO's statutory authority which had a far-reaching effect on the agency's organization, staff, and scope of activity. The changes in the GAO evaluation role have been especially sweeping. The forces behind them are plentiful and complex. Some may have been an inevitable function of natural growth and a changing environment, while others have been the product of more deliberate legislative action.

A review of GAO's transformation from an auditing agency to its broader current role might best start with the evolving congressional mandate. Comptroller General Elmer Staats, who took over direction of the GAO in 1966, was more than cooperative in transforming the role of the agency; but the two laws instrumental in pushing GAO into an expanded role were the Legislative Reorganization Act of 1970 and the Congressional Budget and Impoundment Control Act of 1974.

Under the 1970 act, GAO's responsibilities were extended considerably beyond the traditional financial and management auditing. GAO was required to standardize budget and fiscal data in coordination with the newly-designated Office of Management and Budget (the former Bureau of the Budget) and the

Department of the Treasury. The Act also required GAO to evaluate results of programs and to develop the capacity for preparing cost-benefit studies. It underlined the increased importance Congress attached to an aggressive evaluation role for GAO and removed any element of choice that the agency may have had in the matter. This new direction marked a distinct shift away from a preoccupation with auditing and towards a greater emphasis on evaluating programs and the effect produced by government spending.

The Congressional Budget and Impoundment Control Act of 1974 reinforced and articulated further the evaluation role of GAO by providing for an easier flow of budget and fiscal data as well as specific program information. More specifically, it authorized GAO to set up an office for program evaluation and review to help GAO assume a leadership role in legislative branch evaluation by requiring the agency, through the office, to: assist congressional committees, the Congressional Research Service, and other GAO divisions doing evaluation, and to recommend general strategies and tactics for carrying out program evaluations.

In 1972, the GAO divisions based on the executive structure were abolished and replaced by six functional divisions. Prior to this change GAO studied each department's programs separately, although analysis occasionally did cross departmental lines. After the reorganization and the concomitant concentration on functional areas, appropriate crossing of department jurisdictions was considerably easier. At the subdivision level, though, work remains organized along agency lines.

Some important behind-the-scene shifts accompanied the formal changes that culminated in the 1972 reorganization. In 1969, the Comptroller General began putting more emphasis on system analysis and operations research. This interest was partly a carryover from the Programming, Planning and Budgeting System and Management by Objective strategies aimed at systematizing federal management and decisionmaking that were in vogue at the time. But Comptroller General Staats also planned a broader, more sophisticated role for GAO in program evaluation.

It was recognized that achieving this goal would require GAO to upgrade its capabilities markedly. The Congressional Budget and Impoundment Control Act generated more impetus to diversify the qualifications of GAO personnel. The Act called for intensive budget analysis, which Congress was not then equipped to handle. Anticipating the demand, GAO created a new Office of Budget and Program Analysis, assigning it the task of developing a capability for extensive quantitative and policy analysis—much headier stuff than checking vouchers and auditing financial transactions, to be sure.[21] However, the budget analysis duties were temporary. After less than a year, the new Congressional Budget Office took over the tasks. Having been relieved of budget analysis, the GAO strengthened its policy analysis role by channeling more resources into program evaluation techniques.

Another change in the GAO structure and operations was the adoption in 1975 of the lead division mechanism.[22] It was introduced to serve as a clearinghouse for activities that do not fall neatly into a single GAO division, but straddle two or more, either because broad issues or two or more government agencies are involved. One division is assigned prime responsibility for an activity that cuts across GAO divisional structure. The mechanism has been instrumental in filling in the cracks left by the shift from an agency to a function orientation, and has facilitated the investigation and evaluation of cross-cutting policy areas.

GAO proves the theory that organizational structures can change more frequently and quickly than the people who fill them. In 1972, 0.2 percent of GAO's professional workforce were classified as social scientists, compared with 6 percent six years later when only half of new hires were accountants and auditors. However, even in 1978, nearly two out of every three professional staff members were still accountants and auditors.

---

21. *1976 Budget: Alternatives and Analysis,* prepared by a Special Congressional Staff Working Group under the direction of Samuel H. Cohn (Washington: General Accounting Office, 1975).

22. Comptroller General of the United States, *Annual Report 1975* (Washington: Government Printing Office, 1976), p. 6.

GAO has brought in some outsiders at the top since 1970. Prior to that time, practically all middle and upper management positions were filled from within GAO, and they were virtually all accountants or auditors. During the 1970s, an increasing proportion of top-level vacancies has been filled by outsiders, including social scientists, psychologists, and other professionals needed for the new GAO role.

Because of the complexity and also, no doubt, the political hazards of social program evaluation, GAO relies extensively on consultants to help bolster its in-house expertise and to help give the GAO products credibility. They are brought in at a relatively low cost to augment specific skill shortages in GAO and to bring a fresh perspective to subjects under analysis.

GAO officials prefer consultants to contractors because they cost less, and because they permit more control by GAO over the end product. Consultants are paid only for the time they work. They typically are engaged in projects already planned by GAO in which basic parameters have been established, or they appraise completed drafts. They act as sounding boards and critics for ideas that have already been circulated in GAO, help to maintain the professional standards of agency work, and provide an independent perspective on the problems under examination. Unlike contractors, they do not provide a final report, evaluation, or study design.

Officials also feel that they are more likely to get frank judgments from consultants. Since federal personnel practices impose a limit on the amount of work consultants can do for GAO in any one year, consultants cannot become too dependent on this work. Hence they are more likely to take an independent position than is often the case in the executive branch where agencies and contractors develop long term relationships.

In contrast, GAO has used contractors sparingly in evaluating social programs, in the belief that by using its own staff it can keep better control over methodology and findings and can better assure an acceptable evaluation. It prefers to rely on its own staff, even to the point of sacrificing time and money to achieve thoroughness and credibility. In the 1969 study of the Office of Economic Opportunity, GAO did contract for independent analyses of selected programs and an across-the-board review of similar executive branch studies. Contractors also reviewed the adequacy of the information systems used in program operation, and in some cases interviewed program participants.[23] However, this evaluation was exceptional. GAO turned to outside help because the terrain was unfamiliar. It was also probably necessary to give GAO's evaluation more credibility—GAO was not famous for the quality of its social scientists and, therefore, an internal evaluation of OEO programs might have been suspect. Nevertheless, in that case, as in the few others where GAO used contractors, the outside contributions were subsumed in the final report as a GAO product. This practice can be contrasted to executive agencies which routinely spend millions of dollars for outside evaluations that are signed, sealed, and delivered as final products, with a minimum of structured intervention by government officials.

The GAO preference for consultants over contractors also reflects certain practical considerations. Procurement procedures for contracts over $10,000 are complex and time consuming. When GAO decides to contract, it usually solicits outside help for relatively small pieces of larger studies; contracts over $25,000 are rare. When executive agencies are routinely soliciting bids for studies costing ten times that amount and more, GAO finds relatively few evaluators competing to do its jobs. On the other hand, short term reviews and outside commentaries can be handled by busy social scientists on a consulting basis, and these pay enough for shorter periods of time to make it worth their while.

The Quality of GAO's Evaluation

With a staff in excess of 5,300 persons, GAO is by far the largest of the congressional support staffs. The combined staffs of the

---

23. Comptroller General of the United States, *Review of Economic Opportunity Programs* (Washington: Government Printing Office, 1969), p. 3.

Congressional Research Service, the Office of Technology Assessment, and the Congressional Budget Office are out-numbered five-to-one by GAO's. GAO has a long standing reputation for reliability and integrity—the ideal watchdog. But the field of social program evaluation is a new one. While Comptroller General Staats was drawn into it willingly, indeed eagerly, many of the middle management and some top management personnel had to be dragged into the uncertain art of evaluation. Trained accountants find the work soft and the bottom line disturbingly ambiguous, if not illusive.

The strength of GAO's performance has rested partly on its past reputation as an objective overseer, but much more on its ability to adapt to a more complex and politically contentious branch of analysis. GAO has made organizational adaptations. New leadership has shifted the emphasis of its work and it is acquiring a different kind of professional staff to handle a different kind of job. In short, faced with new responsibilities, GAO has changed. But has the change enabled GAO to serve congressional decisionmaking needs better?

GAO's location in the congressional branch imparts a distinctive quality to its evaluation. In response to congressional inquiries, Comptroller General Staats has spelled out the respective role of GAO and the executive agencies in program evaluation:

> It is our view that program evaluation is a fundamental part of effective program administration. The responsibility, therefore, rests initially upon the responsible agencies. However, in our opinion, the executive agencies too frequently issue reports without adequate consideration of congressional needs. . . . The GAO can help to identify these needs for consideration by the agencies.

> The GAO can assess the objectivity and validity of agency studies. . . . We believe the Congress and GAO, as an arm of Congress, should also have capability to make evaluations of programs. The GAO reviews and

evaluations of programs should not, however, supplant the agencies' responsibilities in this area.[24]

At one level of analysis, the effectiveness of the job GAO does evaluating government social programs hinges upon the methodological adequacy of its work and the relevance and utility of the findings. But evaluation is not GAO's sole function. GAO is first and foremost a congressional support agency. Because of that, GAO's evaluation activities are constrained by the reality that they must meet the particular needs of the Congress, not of program administrators or social scientists. Methodological correctness may at times have to be sacrificed to the imperatives of timeliness and to the need to pass judgments even when there is inadequate information for the formulation of sound evaluations.

In the evaluation of social programs, the General Accounting Office labors under the handicaps that staff members who do the work are, for the most part, not professionally trained social scientists. But what they lack in technical know-how and depth of program experience, GAO evaluators can often make up for with the scope of their experience, abundant resources, and investigative authority. The variety of experience many GAO evaluators have gained is useful in a legislative branch setting. Given the range of demands upon GAO, breadth of experience is probably more important than depth. Nonetheless, considering resources available to GAO, the agency should be able to strike a better balance between the employment of generalists and specialists.

The art of social program evaluation, primitive as it is, has progressed in the last several years. Compared to other social program evaluations, GAO's efforts are sometimes marked by a lack of methodological polish and by inadequate technical understanding of important program features and context. The sampling methods GAO employs in identifying particular projects for study and in collecting program data are sometimes open to serious question.

---

24. Comptroller General of the United States in a letter to the Chairman of the Joint Economic Committee on Congressional Operations, U.S. Congress, August 8, 1974.

The executive agencies that are the subject of GAO's investigations frequently attack GAO findings on methodological grounds. Although the criticisms are self-serving, they are not unfounded. For example, HEW officials, reacting to a critical GAO evaluation of compensatory education, questioned the validity of GAO's criticism with charges of improper sample selection, insufficient sample size, incomplete data collection, and faulty data analysis.[25]

Department of Labor officials challenged the findings of a GAO evaluation of summer youth employment programs also on the basis of its weak methodology and faulty process of inference.[26] As in the case of the HEW compensatory education program, Labor's officials cited their own evaluations that covered larger samples and presented a markedly different picture of program effectiveness.[27]

Given the potential impact of any GAO evaluation, findings have to be qualified and recommendations have to be made with caution where the methodological underpinnings or sampling procedures are weak. But this presents a dilemma for the GAO. Required to respond to congressional requests, GAO must sometimes settle for evaluations based on weak methods on the grounds that it is better than no review at all. The GAO evaluation of compensatory education was undertaken because HEW evaluations were not complete and the Congress was demanding an assessment of program performance. But the evaluation of the summer youth employment program was undertaken despite the fact that a number of DOL assessments of the same program were already underway at the time and scheduled to be completed

25. *Departments of Labor and Health, Education and Welfare Appropriations for 1977,* Part 5, U.S. Congress, House Appropriations Committee (Washington: Government Printing Office, 1976), pp. 99-101.

26. Comptroller General of the United States, "More Effective Management is Needed to Improve the Quality of the Summer Youth Employment Program" (Washington: General Accounting Office, 1979).

27. Robert Taggart, Comments on the General Accounting Office Draft Report, "More Effective Management is Needed to Improve the Quality of the Summer Youth Employment Program," Office of Youth Programs, U.S. Department of Labor, February 12, 1979.

before GAO's. GAO made reference in its review to the other evaluations, but neither critiqued them nor utilized any of their findings.

Where the GAO work merely clutters the landscape with one more opinion of suspect value, it is dubious whether its contribution helps Congress. Where GAO evaluations are the only assessments of programs, GAO ought to state explicitly the limits on inferences that may be drawn from its assessment. To do otherwise is to invite unwarranted extrapolations and imperil legitimate findings.

Aside from in-house resource constraints that impinge on the methodological and substantive sophistication of GAO's work, there is an important institutional constraint. Being in the legislative branch, GAO is removed from the program operation perspective and advantages that go with that perspective. It cannot readily manipulate variables or gear program management and information collection to its evaluation needs. Nor can the GAO evaluators actively participate in program design or operations as do their counterparts in the executive branch. They are, at best, remote observers and, indeed, are frequently considered intruders; they work without enjoying the welcome mat that is laid out for executive evaluators. The most marked disadvantage GAO evaluators work under occurs in social program evaluation activities. Executive agency evaluators can design the program to support evaluation objectives and can monitor its entire life. In contrast, the GAO role in such experiments, as in other programs, is that of an outsider. For example, while Mathematica staff, under contract with HEW, were directly involved in setting up and operating the New Jersey Graduated Work Incentive program, GAO staff came in after the fact to review what had been done, comment on technical aspects of the design, and draw their own policy conclusions from the evidence available to them.

GAO evaluators do not have the same flexibility or opportunity for cooperation and interaction with program staff and clientele as executive branch evaluators. In trying to measure the effect of the HEW compensatory education program on academic achievement, they relied exclusively on available student records, which were incomplete and not designed to assess these effects. In contrast, HEW evaluators were able to utilize their own battery of tests, administer them to program enrollees, control groups, and a cross section of other students. They were also able to specify the timing of additional data that were to be collected. Their data were designed to answer their questions, while the data GAO had to use were not.[28]

Self-imposed constraints also affect the quality of GAO's work. Hoping to achieve independence by maintaining distance from and minimizing interference with program operations, GAO evaluators find themselves frequently building analyses upon only the data that are available from existing records. The data are not always appropriate or reliable for the purpose of answering questions put to GAO. This dogged insistence that its work be original has costs that may not actually be balanced out by the presumed benefits. Resources are wasted reinventing the wheel, and while GAO can vouch for its work as far as it goes, the work is inevitably restricted because the analysts cannot hope to develop comprehensive pictures from limited program records. In a review of programs for migrants and in a study of public service employment programs, the GAO failed to draw on the wealth of available literature on the subjects.

The recently established Program Analysis Division has broken this mold, showing a great willingness to review and synthesize findings from other literature. Its analyses, where they focus on a particular program, go further in speculating on future program impacts and policies in the program area than do those of other divisions.[29] But the work of the division is unique, not typifying the style or substance elsewhere in GAO. Furthermore, analysts in this division frequently do not evaluate particular programs in terms of the specific laws and regulations governing their

---

28. *Departments of Labor and Health, Education and Welfare Appropriations for 1977,* Part 5, p. 101.

29. Comptroller General of the United States, *Section 236 Rental Housing—An Evaluation With Lessons for the Future* (Washington: General Accounting Office, 1978).

implementation, instead focusing on policy areas and future options that encompass a number of laws.[30]

By insisting on preserving its independence and, in particular, failing to adequately acknowledge other literature and incorporate it where appropriate, the GAO divisions that do the vast majority of the social program evaluations may be forcing their work into a strait jacket that reduces the effectiveness of their work. GAO tends to ignore the legislative and administrative agendas behind social legislation and oversimplify the reality in which social programs are implemented. The work rarely questions the practicality of congressional mandates and pays too little attention to the inevitable difficulties inherent in the implementation of social policies.

The insistence upon independence for financial auditing is, of course, justified. But elsewhere, the limitations this puts on GAO reduce the usefulness of its products. The benefit of independence in evaluating the complexities and nuances of intricate social programs is ambiguous at best. As Selma Mushkin has observed: ". . . in the strength of its isolation from Government, [GAO] may also find it is removed from the realities of governments, or even in its isolation, produce an environment hostile to change."[31]

In addition to the problems caused by its isolation, GAO's work has also been marked by unimaginative analyses that sometimes oversimplify reality. Although there have been significant improvements recently, much evaluation has taken legislative rhetoric literally and judged agency performance on the basis of vague or unrealistic legislative goals. GAO evaluators have frequently made no attempt to assess the lofty aspirations of lawmakers in light of realistic, operational impediments faced by administrators. Their analyses sometimes fail to come to grips with the legislative and administrative problems at the core of the

---

30. Comptroller General of the United States, *Inconsistencies in Retirement Age: Issues and Implications* (Washington: General Accounting Office, 1978); and *An Evaluation of the Use of the Transfer Income Model—TRIM—to Analyze Welfare Programs* (Washington: General Accounting Office, 1977).

31. Selma J. Mushkin, in *Legislative Oversight and Program Evaluation,* pp. 232-233.

social initiatives. They have recommended fine adjustments within the confines of assumption-laden legislation, but failing to see the forest for the trees, have not done a good job of assessing the validity of these assumptions.

In a 1972 review of federal employment and training programs, GAO evaluators reported that the Neighborhood Youth Corps, a program established under the Economic Opportunity Act of 1964, was not achieving the legislative objective of reducing the high school dropout rate. While the analysis recognized the fact that the dropout problem was significantly more complex than the Neighborhood Youth Corps could address, the GAO evaluators based their assessment on how well program results conformed to the literal goals of the enabling legislation.[32] Similarly, in analyzing other antipoverty employment and training efforts, GAO placed more emphasis on the letter than the spirit of legislative mandates. Its assessments were mechanical comparisons between program records and statutory requirements. Evaluators paid scant attention to the program environment and the host of conditions affecting the program and its participants.[33]

The General Accounting Office has made, however, considerable progress on this front. The quality of its analysis has improved in recent years and shows promise of continued progress. In a 1974 review of activities under the antirecessionary job creation program, GAO analysts cited the congressional rhetoric, but went on to examine the conditions and practical obstacles faced by employment projects.[34] In its review of federal programs for migrant and seasonal farm workers, the GAO examined the needs of the target population and made an

---

32. Comptroller General of the United States, *Federal Manpower Training Programs: GAO Conclusions and Observations* (Washington: General Accounting Office, February 17, 1972).

33. Comptroller General of the United States, *Effectiveness and Administrative Efficiency of the Concentrated Employment Program Under Title IB of the Economic Opportunity Act of 1964: St. Louis, Missouri* (Washington: General Accounting Office, November 20, 1969).

34. Comptroller General of the United States, *The Emergency Employment Act: Placing Participants in Nonsubsidized Jobs and Revising Hiring Requirements* (Washington: General Accounting Office, March 29, 1974).

imaginative assessment of how the programs were affecting the intended beneficiaries.[35] In much the same vein, a more recent GAO report of public service employment programs reviewed the unemployment problems these programs seek to address and the local forces with which they must contend. It assessed the impact of the programs in their real-life environment and indicated how improvements could be made.[36]

Effects in the Legislative Branch

Considering GAO's mission to assist the Congress, its overall impact ought to be measured primarily in terms of the effects that its evaluations have on policy and legislation. In the distinctively political environment of the legislative branch, GAO offers nonpolitical support, striving to provide objective and independent evidence of program performance. Yet to many observers, its evaluations of social programs appear to have had little appreciable impact in swaying opinions or changing the course of policy. Some of the reasons lie in GAO and some in the structure of the Congress.

Within GAO, there is a persistent tendency to confine recommendations to minor issues involving incremental changes. A typical recommendation urged greater reliance on elementary school facilities in allocating funds for adult education. Another recommendation sought to improve the transferability of findings from an experimental housing allowance program to other housing programs. None of these recommendations was world shaking; most suggested technical improvement in policy execution and program administration. One extensive list of recommendations dealt with upgrading the administration of vocational education programs at all levels of government. Another offered technical changes in vocational rehabilitation legislation to bring it in line with policy established in other

---

35. Comptroller General of the United States, *Impact of Federal Programs to Improve the Living Conditions of Migrant and Other Seasonal Farmworkers* (Washington: General Accounting Office, February 6, 1973).

36. Comptroller General of the United States, *More Benefits to Jobless Can Be Attained in Public Service Employment* (Washington: General Accounting Office, April 7, 1977).

educational legislation. Some of the recommendations are so obvious as to be unnecessary; some urge actions that agencies have already taken. In an evaluation of a bilingual education program, agencies accepted the recommendations while objecting to the analysis leading up to them.

Even where GAO is inclined to offer bolder policy suggestions, Congress may be reluctant to heed the advice. This is sometimes inevitable, not only because GAO is still new to a game in which the competition is keen, but also because Congress is not short of paid and unpaid, formal and voluntary, advisors and lobbyists. Executive agencies, public interest groups, and constituents are constantly vying for the opportunity to present their views. Members of Congress are not accustomed to asking GAO for policy advice, and, given the competition, the GAO is likely to remain on the sidelines when decisions are made.

By one count, Congress acted on only 17 recommendations made by GAO in the social area over a three-year period. All were directed at improving aspects of program management; none reflected findings about basic program impact or involved changes in policy.[37] However, an assessment of GAO effectiveness on the basis of direct congressional responses to its recommendations would be misleading. Congress watchers might argue that action on legislative recommendations is an inadequate indicator for judging any group's effectiveness.[38] Indeed, Congress rarely acts on recommendations from any single source. Furthermore, GAO is rarely included in the decisionmaking process. If GAO's evaluation work has not been eagerly received by Congress, the reason may be that Congress, in the past, has not pursued its oversight responsibilities effectively. Emphasizing the passage of new legislation, Congress has expended little effort in monitoring programs or checking whether early policy has been appropriate. "Congress is oriented to the future, not to the past, so there is a chronic neglect of its oversight role."[39]

37. Comptroller General of the United States, Annual Reports for 1975, 1976, and 1977 (Washington: General Accounting Office), p. 13, pp. 12-17, and pp. 9-15, respectively.

38. *Legislative Oversight and Program Evaluation, op. cit.*

39. Allen Schick, "Evaluating Evaluation: A Congressional Perspective," in *Legislative Oversight and Program Evaluation*, p. 348.

Another factor that impinges on GAO's work is the coziness between congressional committees and executive agencies. The interest in oversight notwithstanding, senior members of committees or subcommittees may get defensive about legislation they have sponsored and may not be inclined to welcome GAO's criticisms. As a result, GAO evaluators are often left out in the cold when they lack rapport with, and access to, senior members.[40]

The story of GAO's contribution to legislative oversight is not entirely bleak, however. Aside from the few—but interesting—cases when GAO social program evaluations have had an immediate influence, GAO work does, in conjunction with other evidence, make a difference in the long run. It often spurs interests, develops leads, or establishes facts that serve as jumping-off points for committee staff work.[41] Perhaps the most encouraging evidence of congressional interest in GAO evaluations is the active encouragement it is given by committee staffs. Although GAO is not the first choice to evaluate social programs, the consensus of opinion is that its mere presence exerts a strong influence on executive evaluators to do a more credible job.

In the separation of powers between the legislative branch and the executive branch, the latter has traditionally assumed the lion's share of program evaluation. But that is changing. The Congressional Budget and Impoundment Control Act of 1974, which included a mandate for vigorous congressional oversight, was spurred largely in response to perceived executive abuses and a lack of legislative evaluation capabilities.[42] The sudden interest in "sunset" laws and the revived interest in zero-based budgeting reflect similar sentiment. Interest in legislative oversight seems to be on the upswing. While the effectiveness of GAO evaluations has been limited, there are encouraging signs for the future.

Effects in the Executive Branch

While GAO was established to serve the Congress, the fallout of its evaluations upon executive agencies cannot be ignored. Indeed,

---

40. *Ibid.*, p. 187.

41. *Ibid.*, p. 187.

42. *Congressional Quarterly Weekly Report,* April 28, 1973, pp. 1013-1018.

in addition to evaluating at the behest of committees and members of Congress, the GAO may also respond to requests of agency heads to review their operations. However, few agency heads ask GAO to evaluate their programs. Instead, the primary vehicles of GAO influence are the recommendations made in GAO reports and the subtle "threat" of GAO's presence acting to keep administrators clean.

Virtually all GAO program evaluations include recommendations to program officials. Although the recommendations are aimed at clarifying congressional mandates and improving policy implementation, the GAO too frequently restates the provisions of the law establishing the program. It is not surprising, therefore, that following a path of least resistance, agencies usually concur with GAO recommendations, while seldom changing their policies or plans. The agencies assume that once the report is filed, GAO will not return for awhile and that, also, there will be no organized follow-up on the GAO recommendations. This is not to deny that the GAO reviews are sometimes especially perceptive and constructive. But, as a rule, they make no new discoveries and are modest in comparison to the more comprehensive evaluations conducted by the agencies.

GAO's administrative recommendations are much more carefully heeded. In its historical field of expertise—program and financial management—GAO has brought unique talents to bear and its findings have had marked influence. It has been especially effective in analyzing the administrative problems that were immobilizing the federal employees disability compensation program, and was the prime mover in forcing passage of the Federal Employees Compensation Act of 1974. GAO was also instrumental in identifying administrative snags in the food stamp program, Aid to Families with Dependent Children, and the Supplemental Security Income program.

The specter of the "watchdog" looking over the executive branch shoulder is also important. In the opinion of some executive branch observers—program personnel and evaluators alike—the most compelling effect of GAO evaluations is not in their actual, but their potential content. More bluntly, GAO hangs as Damocles' sword ready to fall on the heads of program administrators and agency-supported evaluators. Executive personnel frequently question the soundness of GAO evaluations and rely more on their agencies' own comprehensive studies. But the GAO acts as a check; there is little likelihood of an agency evaluation being taken seriously if it contradicts GAO findings, crude as they may be. It also discourages evaluators from settling for a whitewash to avoid GAO exposure. "If bureaucrats anticipate that their actions will be inspected by other units of the bureaucracy, by the Congress, and perhaps by the courts, they are more likely to act with a sense of responsibility."[43]

On the whole, however, GAO's contribution to the formulation and implementation of social policy has been minimal. The agency has lacked substantive program knowledge and adequate understanding of the environment in which social programs operate. Measures to upgrade and broaden staff quality take time, and experienced technical personnel in analytical areas are always in short supply. Finally, GAO still has a reputation as a "keep 'em honest" watchdog. It remains dominated by an "accountant mentality" for various reasons, including tradition, the preponderance of accountants on the staff, and the fact that even the best social science evaluation is a politically and intellectually hazardous enterprise about which the experienced and prudent GAO leaders are understandably cautious. Legislators are accustomed to GAO doing financial auditing and have traditionally turned to other agencies and private experts for the evaluation of social programs. With the rising prominence of the Congressional Budget Office, GAO is still usually not their first resort when a program evaluation is needed.

THE CONGRESSIONAL RESEARCH SERVICE

An Expanding Mission

Established in 1914 as the Legislative Reference Service, the Congressional Research Service (CRS) is the senior congressional

---

43. Morris S. Ogul, *Congress Oversees the Bureaucracy* (Pittsburgh: University of Pittsburgh Press, 1976), p. 192.

support agency. It is unique, acting as a nonpartisan, scholarly agency also thoroughly involved in virtually all aspects of lawmaking. In contrast to the General Accounting Office, which has its own accounting and fiscal management responsibilities apart from its legislative support tasks, CRS is entirely an appendage to the Congress.

In the evaluation of social programs, other features also mark the Congressional Research Service as unique. No stranger to the social sciences, CRS has for years relied on the work of academic scholars and their familiarity with federal social initiatives. The CRS staff has included prominent social scientists since its precursor, the Legislative Reference Service, broadened its emphasis during the 1940s beyond indexing and referencing to include all aspects of federal policy analysis. CRS now has greater depth and scope of experience in the social science disciplines than ever before. But the agency's role in evaluating social programs is a limited one. CRS staff are well-equipped to analyze and digest the findings of social program evaluations, and do so in the normal course of their work. They are not technically responsible, however, for the direct evaluation of federal social programs. In a seminar on congressional oversight and evaluation, a former CRS top officer made note of the ambiguity:

> There is really no significant distinction between providing policy analysis for pending legislation and providing analytical assistance for legislative oversight and evaluation. These classically discrete legislative functions are in fact, part of a "push-pull" continuous process.[44]

Although CRS has recognized that the distinction between policy analysis and evaluation is not very useful, Congress has decreed that GAO should be responsible for program evaluation, and CRS for the formulation of policy options. Hence, CRS cannot formally classify its work as evaluation. Nonetheless, CRS

---

44. Norman Beckman, "Congressional Research Service: Resources for Oversight and Evaluation," in *Legislative Oversight and Program Evaluation,* p. 71.

is an important determinant of whether program evaluations do or do not influence the course of legislation.

The roots of the original Legislative Reference Service (LRS) go back in history to its parent agency, the Library of Congress, established in 1800 to support the work of Congress by providing facts and information to the lawmakers. Library staff have worked with members of Congress on the floors of both houses and in committee chambers with committee staff. They have provided information and references on a great variety of information needed by the Congress, researched the facts behind legislation, and ferreted out legal precedents. This broad mission lent coherence to the Library's work and met the needs of Congress for more than a century.

However, as the information needs of Congress increased and grew more complex, Congress required a more specialized reference service to keep track of and assist in its manifold operations. Hence, the Legislative Reference Service was formed in 1914 "to enable the Librarian of Congress to employ competent persons to prepare such indexes, digests, and compilations of law as may be required for Congress and other official use."[45]

The demand for the new agency's services grew slowly through the early 1940s. Most of its work was directed towards locating and referencing information on issues before the Congress, and compiling, abstracting, and indexing statutes. After World War II, Congress further expanded the responsibilities of the federal government. The social programs initiated in the depression, the gigantic military undertaking during the second World War, and the leading role America took in postwar world affairs all contributed to the enlargement of the national government.

This growth required a corresponding growth in congressional staff support. Simple reference work and legislative indices did not satisfy the pressing congressional information needs. Congress needed more comprehensiveness than the piecemeal analyses then available to evaluate the ramifications of congressional actions

---

45. *Annual Report of the Congressional Research Service of the Library of Congress for the Fiscal Year 1971* (Washington: Government Printing Office, 1972), p. 5.

and identify and assess the impacts of government programs. The job was larger and more complicated than it had been before and members of Congress and their personal and committee staffs could not do it alone. Staff members were spread too thinly and were frequently selected for their political abilities, rather than for their substantive expertise in policy areas.

The Legislative Reorganization Act of 1946 represented an attempt to adapt Library of Congress services to a larger legislative role. It broadened the responsibility of LRS, authorizing the Librarian of Congress to appoint specialists to analyze and evaluate the substance of legislative proposals. The forward-looking policy analysis role was seen as a logical adjunct to the "watchdog" audit and review activities of GAO. GAO was assigned the task of ensuring that the will of Congress was executed, while LRS was to anticipate and illuminate the implications of prospective congressional actions.

For the next 24 years, the LRS mission remained relatively intact as the agency slowly expanded. Staff were added in a number of substantive areas to examine emerging issues. A Congressional Reference Division was established to do basic reference work utilizing readily available resources. This "new" addition, providing a specialized channel for responding to requests for data and straightforward factual inquiries, actually reemphasized the original LRS mission. However, it served also to demarcate more clearly the function of policy analysis and sophisticated research.

The Legislative Reorganization Act of 1970 accelerated the expansion of the LRS and renamed the agency the Congressional Research Service, leaving it in the Library of Congress but making it more autonomous. The 1970 law also laid the groundwork for greatly expanding the size of the service.[46] By the end of fiscal 1978, the number of CRS budgeted positions had more than doubled to over 800. Annual appropriations nearly quadrupled over the same period, rising to more than $23 million in fiscal

---

46. *Report of the Committee on Rules of H.R. 17654, Legislative Reorganization Act of 1970* (Washington: Government Printing Office, 1970), p. 19.

1978. The growth of CRS, like that of the General Accounting Office, no doubt reflects the expanded oversight role of the Congress and greater recognition among members of Congress of the need for research and evaluation capabilities independent of the executive branch.

Two-thirds of the CRS staff are in the research divisions and work primarily on substantive research and analysis. Twenty percent of the staff are engaged in handling routine information requests, and the balance are in administrative positions. The CRS is broad-based and rich in experience. In fiscal 1978, about two-thirds were professionals, embracing almost every imaginable discipline, with the vast majority having advanced degrees. Some have national reputations as established experts in their fields.

Administration Structure

The present structure of the research divisions has remained virtually unchanged since it was set up along university department lines to carry out the mandates of the Legislative Reorganization Act of 1946. As the scope of congressional committees does not precisely correspond with that of executive agencies, the CRS structure has been effective in pulling together pieces of policy that have been scattered throughout the government. For example, one study found federally funded education programs in 23 executive agencies and education affairs handled by 26 congressional committees.[47] With an organizational structure that cuts across both the executive and legislative decision lines and yet requires relatively few divisions, CRS has succeeded in focusing the many disparate perspectives existing within its policy work.

The central purpose of the Legislative Reorganization Act of 1970 was to improve and expand the ability of the Congress to discharge more systematically and comprehensively its oversight responsibilities. The CRS was chosen to assist Congress in this

47. *Information Resources and Services Available from the Library of Congress and the Congressional Research Service,* U.S. Congress, House Commission on Information and Facilities (Washington: Government Printing Office, 1976), pp. 92-100.

activity. An alternative that was seriously considered was to add one staff person to each standing committee solely to perform review and oversight tasks. The idea was dropped because new committee staff, it was presumed, would inevitably get involved in other responsibilities. The alternative of creating a new support agency devoted exclusively to oversight was also rejected because of the time a new organization would need to get established and because an oversight capability already existed in the General Accounting Office and the Legislative Reference Service. It was decided than an incremental approach was best, for necessary change was seen as quantitative rather than qualitative.[48]

But quantitative change brought qualitative change as well. The expansion of CRS staff has led to increased specialization. The informal structure and close relationship with many members and staff of the Congress that marked the old CRS has been difficult to preserve in a large organization. By virtue of its increasing size (and its past success), CRS is becoming a bureaucracy. Whether the informality and person-to-person contact that was its hallmark can be preserved remains to be seen.

In contrast to the General Accounting Office, which does much of its work without specific congressional directives, CRS does nearly all its work directly in response to congressional requests. Working hand-in-hand with personal and committee staff, CRS has evolved as a specialized information gathering and analytical resource, geared to respond quickly to routine as well as complex congressional inquiries.

Although there is no hard and fast rule for differentiating the varied kinds of work that the Congressional Research Service does, one crude but useful distinction that can be made is between routine inquiries and requests for original research and analysis. The former constitutes the vast majority of over three hundred thousand inquiries CRS received in fiscal 1978. Sixty-three percent were answered within a day, 82 percent in five days, and 83 percent in ten days—a pattern which has remained fairly constant

---

48. *Report of the Committee on Rules of H.R. 17654, Legislative Reorganization Act of 1970*, p. 1720.

over recent years. In terms of numbers, most of the inquiries handled by CRS are requests for facts. The typical responses, handled by a special reference division, involve verifying information, collecting bibliographies, or photocopying library materials.

CRS's major research projects are comprehensive examinations of important policy issues by interdivisional teams. These command the most staff resources and probably have the greatest policy impact. They are undertaken in response to committee requests or in anticipation of committee needs. Although reports requested by individual members certainly are not ignored, those prepared for committees are assigned higher priority by CRS staffers who view the latter assignments as an important means of bringing CRS expertise to bear on legislative policymaking.

CRS evaluations of social programs are conducted chiefly by the Education and Public Welfare and the Economics Divisions, which are concerned with economic analysis, employment, education, vocational rehabilitation, housing, income support, public health, collective bargaining, and economic development. The issues involved in such broad subjects do not always fall neatly into one division and so, in dealing with them, staff from different divisions work freely together. For example, "redlining"—the restrictive lending practices of many mortgage institutions—is a volatile political issue important to national housing policy. Yet, because national action against redlining touches a number of government policy areas, and because some of the staff knowledgeable about redlining are not economists, it is handled by public administration experts and political scientists. Similarly, the Education and Public Welfare Division, rather than the Economics Division, coordinates econometric studies of alternative income support programs because of their close linkage to welfare reform policies. The exact division of labor defies consistent logic and cannot be depicted by most organizational charts, but the easy cooperation of staff from different divisions is effective in broadening the scope and strengthening the quality of work.

Many important subjects do not fit neatly into the categories of traditional academic disciplines. In working on welfare reform and other broad issues, CRS establishes interdivisional teams. The use of such teams received special emphasis in the Legislative Reorganization Act of 1970, which sought to strengthen the comprehensive policy analysis capabilities of the legislative branch. The workload of the Economics Division and the Education and Public Welfare Division is large and growing. Between them, in 1978, the two divisions responded to 26,000 inquiries. Although the great majority were routine requests for information that were filled quickly, the volume of longer term studies was the highest ever.

Evaluation in CRS

CRS staff rarely assess program performance. Evaluation is, by their standards, a "backward looking" exercise that is subordinate to CRS emphasis on policy design and analysis. Nonetheless, evaluation, by whatever name it is called, is a major function of CRS. To know where it is going, Congress must know where it has been. Good policy analysis—the examination of alternative courses of action and of their implications—requires an assessment of prior experience. For that purpose, CRS makes much use of evaluations by executive agencies, the General Accounting Office, private organizations and interest groups. CRS examines those evaluations, digests them, and incorporates the conclusions, if not the details, into policy analysis.

An assessment of the job that the Congressional Research Service does in evaluating social programs has to recognize that CRS was established to fill a support role. Although it strives for nonpartisanship, it is very much a part of the congressional decisionmaking process. The legislative milieu is one of turmoil, with abrupt shifts in priorities and the sudden emergence, whether real or imaginary, of pressing new issues as events and circumstances dictate. It is hardly an atmosphere conducive to careful and deliberate academic research. In that setting, much CRS research is a race against time in which thoroughness conflicts with demands for speedy delivery. The fact is, one of the main purposes for setting up CRS was to provide Congress fast service. As time is an overriding consideration on the Hill, CRS must respond quickly to inquiries, no matter how complex. When time is not critical, Congress is more apt to try some source other than CRS.

Neither congressional staffs nor the General Accounting Office can quickly marshal such a wide range of expertise as CRS. Congressional staff are spread too thinly to be able to analyze issues carefully on a regular basis. The rigid emphasis that GAO places on time-consuming investigative field work puts it at a disadvantage, too. In CRS, highly specialized staff can be concentrated in a single issue area. CRS can also use outside organizations and consultants where in-house talent is short. This streamlined research structure is well adapted to the congressional pace, making it very popular. Possibly more than half of all CRS research is conducted on a rush basis when quick, albeit less than thorough, analysis is necessary if the product is to be of any use. Legislative decisions have to be made quickly. The stress on speed raises the question of whether CRS encourages relatively shallow instead of more thorough analyses that might be planned in advance.

There is no simple solution to the dilemma, but the CRS approach has great merit. On the slower moving issues, CRS may help committees to plan hearings, blocking out the major issues or filling gaps in the broader, deeper base of knowledge presented in hearings. In that setting, it is rarely the only source of analysis relied upon by the Congress. Even during the 1974 energy crisis, CRS supplied only a portion of the information and analysis. Many other sources were also employed, and when pressure from special interests delayed final action, closer scrutiny of the major proposals was possible. That kind of haste is rare when social legislation is enacted. Some would argue that congressional action is as slow as social change. Still the legislative process is full of fast turns and sudden decision points. Initial congressional response may be changed and shaped in legislative debate. Different kinds of analysis are persuasive at different times, and varied approaches are needed to meet the needs of members. Regardless of how much fact-finding has preceded congressional action, new analysis and new proposals always arise. This is the kind of situation in which CRS, it is asserted, can be most helpful, although it is hard to pinpoint spots where CRS has been decisive in resolving a major policy issue.

The essential value of the Congressional Research Service's fast responses is to present reasonably unbiased information and analysis adapted to congressional time constraints. When time permits, basic data from a variety of sources are more carefully reported. When time is short, it may be possible only to summarize or extract a few sources. Such varied responses are characteristic of CRS.

In evaluating social programs and policies, CRS has two alternative and complementary procedures: reviewing available literature, and collecting data from operating agencies. Although time may be crucial in determining which methods are employed, it is not the only factor. There are important qualitative distinctions among the sources that also determine how CRS goes about evaluating social programs.

Literature searches are the primary source of information for CRS analysts trying to assess social programs and domestic policy. When the Congressional Research Service was established, members of Congress envisioned a research service that would analyze and digest available information and analyses and synthesize them in a balanced examination of the important perspectives bearing on legislative issues. The lawmakers had in mind a service that would do more than collect relevant studies, but would stop short of gathering its own primary data. In an age when the volume of information is as overwhelming as its content, the objective has proven farsighted and enduring. The aim today is to lay out the different perspectives, showing the "facts" and analyzing opposing views. The hope is that the product will help the legislators to reach a balanced view. For example, an examination of the effectiveness of employment and training programs analyzed and summarized a full spectrum of studies of the impact of federal initiatives.[49] The studies had been done by federal executive agencies, research groups, special interest representatives, and scholars. In an evaluation of the Appalachian Regional Commission, CRS analysts relied on a variety of sources for information on the Commission's goals and effectiveness.[50] Much had been written about the Commission, and there was no need for CRS to start an evaluation from scratch.

When available literature on program operations is inadequate, as is often the case with new social programs, CRS is likely to rely on operational data from executive agencies. This information is particularly relevant in evaluating the effectiveness of those social programs that are highly sensitive to changes in the economy. The strain that the 1974-75 recession put on income support programs raised major questions in Congress about appropriate legislative responses. Existing literature was understandably inadequate to shed new light on the problems. To fill the void, CRS analysts relied on executive agency data to determine how well the programs were holding up, and to gain insights into emerging changes in program operations. After evaluating these data, CRS presented its analysis of the situation and examined measures for making adjustments in the income support programs. Ready access to operational data is an important aspect of CRS program evaluation and policy analysis. Without the close executive agency rapport and the opportunity to use operating data as a basis for evaluating policy effectiveness, analytical work in this area would be stale and often useless.

Independence

Although the informal cooperation of CRS and the executive agencies has proven fruitful, it is not without problems. The dependence of the service upon executive sources of information

---

49. Ray Schmitt, *The Effectiveness of Manpower Training Programs: A Compilation of Observations and Conclusions* (Washington: Congressional Research Service, May 29, 1973).

50. John Mitrisin, *A Selective Evaluation of the Appalachian Regional Commission Program* (Washington: Congressional Research Service, March 15, 1973).

raises doubts as to whether the data and analyses that CRS supplies to Congress are tainted with biases of the operating agencies whose activities Congress is attempting to assess.

The independence of the legislative branch in overseeing executive activities has been a recurring issue throughout the history of congressional support agencies in general and the Congressional Research Service in particular. The Legislative Reorganization Act of 1946 reflected the sentiment that the Congress should be able to do its own analysis so that it could independently assess executive performance and achieve a more active role in formulating and analyzing policy options. The analytical capability that CRS began to develop after the 1946 legislation progressed slowly, at best. The burgeoning social programs in the 1960s intensified the issue of legislative independence. Suspicion and mistrust between the two branches were exacerbated under the Nixon administration. Many became convinced that Congress would be at the mercy of the executive branch if it placed excessive trust in agency evaluations and perspectives. It was essential, according to this view, that the legislative branch be able to generate its own data about executive branch performance.

The Legislative Reorganization Act of 1970 and the Congressional Budget and Impoundment Control Act of 1974 enhanced the independence of legislative analysis. These two pieces of legislation laid the foundation for a management information system designed to provide congressional analysts with direct access to certain agency budget and operating data. The laws also stressed the importance of GAO program evaluations and enlarged the staff of CRS, enabling it to conduct more analytical work. The extent of the changes has been more quantitative than qualitative, though. The automated system for retrieving agency budget and program data is not yet fully operational, and it is unlikely to have much impact on CRS evaluations. In a list of priorities prepared by CRS analysts, the use of raw data ranks low. When time is pressing, the analysis of operational details seldom takes precedence over the use of existing evaluations. Because of practical considerations, direct access to operational data will probably continue to contribute less to independent analysis than will the opportunity to discuss with executive evaluators the strengths and weaknesses of their work.

When the data provided by the executive agencies are inadequate or unreliable, CRS can, in theory, turn for help to the General Accounting Office, which is better able to generate data based on its own observations of onsite operations. Yet, in practice, CRS staff rarely use GAO data for their evaluations. GAO collects data for its own specific needs which seldom correspond to those of CRS. Furthermore, when both agencies assess the same program or agency, it is usually for the purpose of producing independent opinions. Consequently, CRS use of GAO data might be self-defeating.

In any event, the operating statistics that GAO produces are often inadequate for depicting current situations and are more dated than the agency figures. Hence, CRS tends to prefer its agency sources. The data are more accessible, suitable, complete, and timely. In short, CRS staff members believe that independent data are not as important as independent analysis.

Getting Outside Help

Contracting out work is a new but growing development at CRS. Outlays increased from $3,000 in 1970 to more than $800,000 in fiscal 1978, contributing significantly to the agency's independence. The number of persons being brought in from the outside on a temporary basis has been increasing as the growing demands on CRS periodically overtax its staff. Rather than trying to enlarge that staff to meet every foreseeable inquiry, the trend has been to contract for specialized services. The rationale is to maintain a solid core of in-house staff for most CRS work and to cope with any overload, and unusual or specialized requests, by contracting. This strategy has been fostered both formally and informally. The Legislative Reorganization Act of 1970 permits CRS to issue contracts without advertising for bids, eliminating a time-consuming and frequently wasteful process. On the informal side, the fairly simple CRS structure and contract review procedures reduce time and red tape. Because of these conditions, rare among federal agencies, CRS can negotiate contracts much more quickly than most executive agencies, preserving its quick response capability.

The reasons for contracting may vary among CRS divisions. The Economics Division relies on contractors for work that its staff can, but are not available to, do. The Education and Public Welfare Division uses them for new ideas or analytical techniques that its staff still lacks. The latter is deeply involved in some highly politicized issues; over the years it has developed closer contacts with the legislative committees than have other CRS divisions because committee members and their staffs heavily rely on it, eager for nonpartisan guidance. Moreover, income maintenance, the financial soundness of the social security system, and the effectiveness of federal measures to deal with social ills are all topics that inspire heated debates. In such areas, the limitations of social science evaluation are keenly felt. New ideas and information are manifestly needed. CRS has turned to consultants and contractors in the hope that they can provide some fresh insights or at least convince Congress of the complexity of the issues.

The growing use of contracted service is becoming an integral part of the agency's response capability. But two forces are at work that may reduce the effectiveness of contracting. The first is the "catch-22"—the built-in hazards of a high volume of contract work. The second is the evil attending the aging of bureaucracies. When contracting was rare, it could be handled with dispatch by short and simple procedures. But as the volume increased, formal and more complex procedures were required so that all requests could be screened systematically for their potential usefulness, economy, and effectiveness. By 1975, handling contracts became a full-time job for a contract officer. While the review procedure is not a tangle of red tape, definite contract procedures have been established, and the entire operation has taken on a formality that was not there in the early 1970s.

Assessing CRS

Virtually the entire mission of the Congressional Research Service is mirrored in the needs of the Congress. As the 1970 reorganization act stated: "Upon request, CRS will supply committees with experts capable of preparing, or assisting in preparing, objective, nonpartisan, in-depth analyses and appraisals of any subject matter. These analyses and appraisals will be directed towards assisting committees. . . ."[51]

Most of the service's substantive reports synthesize and analyze the work of others. It is assumed that findings are selected and presented in a balanced, nonpartisan manner. CRS is supposed to remain pristinely pure, apolitical, fair, and objective. Congress hoped that it would ". . . insulate the analytical phases of program review and policy analysis from political biases and therefore produce a more credible and objective product."[52]

The effectiveness of CRS must be judged largely by the degree of congressional confidence in its work. The agency's managers have duly noted this fact, and periodically they have asked their congressional clients to evaluate CRS work. Although these surveys do not cover all congressional users, do not employ rigorous sampling techniques, and may be partly self-serving, they do provide some insights into client opinions of CRS. The service receives high marks—over 95 percent—for fast and pertinent responses. Less positive though is the finding that CRS does not provide the kind of comprehensive material that 20-25 percent of the members want.

In 1975, CRS expanded the questionnaire to get more detailed responses. Congressional users rated CRS reports on five criteria: thoroughness, clarity, selection, balance, and overall quality. About 80 to 90 percent of the respondents rated CRS high on thoroughness, selection, and balance. Committee staff gave consistently lower marks than members, perhaps because, given

---

51. *Report of the Committee on Rules of H.R. 17654, Legislative Reorganization Act of 1970*, p. 18.

52. *Ibid.*, p. 17.

their specialized responsibilities, they were more inclined to recognize inadequacies in the CRS analyses.[53]

Another important index of CRS work is its degree of objectivity, i.e., does CRS prepare balanced reports that are free of bias and give equal treatment to both (if not all) sides of an issue? To satisfy 535 members of Congress on that score is probably impossible. But CRS received high marks for balance roughly 85 percent of the time from both Democrats and Republicans.[54]

Because of the complexity of the legislative and policymaking processes, it is impossible to isolate the specific impact of CRS evaluative work. Again, the proof of the pudding is in the eating, and some evidence might be gleaned from congressional usage, the agency's sole market test. It is probably fairly safe to assume that congressional users will go back to the CRS sources that it finds helpful. Using this line of reasoning, the available facts indicate that CRS must be doing something right. But the assessment must differentiate between responses to consistent requests and substantive products. The increases in "quickie" requests frequently reflect a response to constituent inquiries and usually require simply supplying a copy of a publication. These requests may be an indicator that more people are writing to their representatives in Congress rather than a test of CRS performance.

The usefulness of CRS can be better judged, therefore, by the rise in analytical work for committees. CRS has been devoting an increasing proportion of its resources to this work. Both the Senate Labor and Human Resources Committee and the House Education and Labor Committee, traditionally heavy users of CRS, have appreciably increased their requests for analytical work.[55]

53. Gary Lee Evans and Dan Melnick, "Report on the Results of the December 1975 Feedback Survey," Congressional Research Service, May 11, 1976.

54. Memorandum from Gary Evans and Dan Melnick to Norman Beckman, Acting Director of the Congressional Research Service, May 11, 1976.

55. Annual Reports of the Congressional Research Service of the Library of Congress, prepared for the Joint Committee on the Library (Washington: Government Printing Office).

This suggests that CRS clients welcome its help in the social policy area. Critics might respond that Congress is so desperate for information that it turns to the readiest source, regardless of its quality. A consensus view would have to be mixed. On the whole, CRS may not provide better information and analysis than anyone else, but it can provide them quickly and reliably. For Congress, ignorance is not bliss, and half a story in time is better than the entire story too late.

4
Evaluation in the Executive Branch

The prime functions of evaluation in the executive branch focus on administration and program operation, rather than on oversight as in the legislative branch. Responsible for implementing the will of Congress, the executive agencies must determine if programs are meeting established objectives and how effective various components are.

However, the purposes of evaluation vary among the executive agencies. They run the range from a search for answers to specific questions to the general advancement of knowledge and ideas. The Office of Management and Budget (OMB) has, from time to time, placed a strong emphasis on the "decision relevance" of evaluations, implying an almost one-to-one correspondence between an evaluation and a particular decision.[1] But this narrow application of evaluation has gained little currency. Evaluation in the executive branch more commonly has the broader function of raising the level of understanding about the impact of social programs.

The evaluation scene in the executive branch is intricate, confusing, and sometimes contradictory. Units with one or another evaluation responsibility saturate every niche of the bureaucracy. To catalog every evaluator or to assemble a complete

---

1. James Morrison, Jr., "Evaluation Management: A Background Paper," Executive Office of the President, Office of Management and Budget, May 1975.

picture of evaluation units and their activities would be nearly impossible and of little value. The Office of Management and Budget discovered just how difficult it is to determine the scope of evaluation activities when it attempted to "standardize" them.[2] Its proposed "general guidance and responsibilities for administration of program evaluation activities within departments and agencies"[3] elicited little interest from program officials. Of course, any such attempt is bound to meet some resistance, but in addition, the arguments against standardizing evaluation formats or management procedures were compelling. OMB defined evaluation narrowly, excluding much that is considered entirely legitimate; the "guidance" offered was so broad as to be useless. In brief, OMB was no more successful than others in clearly defining the scope of evaluation, and its clout proved a poor substitute for intellectual substance. The mandate never got beyond the draft stage and OMB efforts to rationalize evaluation management have been suspended.

Learning from that experience, it is reasonable to conclude that the search for a representative model of social program evaluation in the executive branch is not a rewarding pursuit. Despite some methodological similarities, the variations among agencies and agency components are substantial, and generalizations about evaluation activities in executive departments are of doubtful value.

Four factors visibly affect the role and influence of evaluation in federal agencies: the organizational location, the funding base, the position and power of the people planning evaluation agendas, and the channels for incorporating evaluation findings into policy.

Organizational location and, of course, budgets are particularly useful gauges of the weight assigned to evaluation in an agency. It is important to consider where the evaluation unit is lodged in the hierarchy of authority and the range of functions assigned to it; proximity to managers may enhance its influence on operations

---

2. *Ibid.*

3. Fernando Oaxaca, "Draft OMB Circular on Evaluation of Federal Programs," Executive Office of the President, Office of Management and Budget, November 19, 1975.

while proximity to research may reduce it. While the level of funds available for evaluation is obviously significant, the source of support—in terms of set-asides versus budget line items—may be no less important.

The organizational structure in which planning and managing evaluation take place is a good indicator of its standing. Unlike research, evaluation strives to have some immediate relevance to agency policies, strategies, or tactics, and a direct relationship to agency operations or plans. This requires genuine interaction between program administrators and evaluators, starting with the planning of evaluation projects. Yet, evaluators too frequently fail to involve program managers adequately in their planning, and vice versa.

The ways and extent to which evaluation findings are used are obviously important in determining the nature of evaluation activities. Just as the involvement of program people in the evaluation planning stages is one indicator of how seriously evaluation is taken, so is the willingness of agency decisionmakers to predicate action on evaluation findings.

THE TWO LEADING AGENCIES

The experiences of the Department of Health, Education and Welfare and the Department of Labor offer more than mere case studies. These two departments administer the largest volume of outlays for social program accounting, and comprise 70 percent of the approximately $140 million federal expenditure for social program evaluation in 1977.[4]

HEW's Establishment

The Department of Health, Education and Welfare, with the largest budget and second largest workforce of any department, has a sprawling evaluation establishment which spends approximately $80 million annually. HEW provides so many social

---

4. Statement of Wayne Granquist in *Cost Management and Utilization of Human Resources Program Evaluation, 1977,* U.S. Congress, Senate Committee on Human Resources (Washington: Government Printing Office, 1978), p. 4.

services to American citizens that it is virtually impossible to describe its mission in a single, coherent statement. Its manifold missions reflect piecemeal growth as new legislative mandates have piled upon old. The independence of HEW's individual agencies and the confusion and overlap in their missions shape their evaluation activities in a way that resists organizational rationalization.

Evaluation in HEW crisscrosses lines of jurisdiction and can be highly competitive. Each of the six HEW assistant secretaries has an evaluation office. The Office of Human Development and Education Division focus on planning and budgeting operations, while the Social Security Administration concentrates on research. The degree of centralization varies. In the Office of the Assistant Secretary for Education, one unit is supposed to monitor all education evaluation. Yet, its cooperation with the National Institute of Education and with the evaluation activities of the Office of Education is minimal. In the Public Health Service, most evaluation is conducted by six program agencies which are relatively independent of the central Office of Policy Development and Planning. The Office of Human Development, much smaller than the Public Health Service, also maintains a decentralized operation with each of five program agencies conducting its own evaluations. At the top of this shaky pyramid (it is perhaps more like a pile of gravel), attempting to provide some central guidance and struggling, not too valiantly, to introduce a semblance of administrative order and tidiness, is the Office of the Assistant Secretary for Planning and Evaluation. This office has a nominal veto power over the evaluation plans of agencies but, recognizing the fruitlessness of trying to cast them all in the same mold, has wisely not exercised it. It uses its pivotal position, instead, to execute its own evaluation agenda in areas cutting across organizational lines.

Complicating the jumbled organization of evaluation units are their splintered budgets. With some exceptions, most evaluation funds come from set-aside provisions specified in authorizing legislation. The National Institute of Education funds evaluation from its regular operating budget authorized to support research.

Two agencies in the Office of Human Development fund evaluation from administrative set-asides. The Social Security Administration has no separate budget for evaluation. It is funded, instead, under the rubric of research. Before it was absorbed into the Office of Human Development and the Social Security Administration, the Social and Rehabilitation Service funded evaluation from its research budget, with the Department of Labor and the Community Services Administration providing partial support on several joint programs. The Office of the Assistant Secretary for Planning and Evaluation funds its work by tapping up to 25 percent from agency evaluation budgets.

Advocates of evaluation argue that legislative set-aside provisions assure financing for their activities. However, the full amount of the available set-aside is rarely expended. The Public Health Service, for example, has seldom used more than a third of the available set-aside; in recent years, it has used only a fifth. Underutilization of evaluation resources is mainly attributable to a lack of staff for monitoring projects and assessing the findings. As set-asides cannot be used to hire more staff due to congressionally imposed personnel ceilings and administrative policy, the volume of evaluation has been arrested below prescribed funding levels and certainly falls short of achieving the congressional and administration objectives of evaluation.

However, even if the full evaluation set-asides were spent, it is not certain that a marked increase in genuine evaluation would result. Given the variety of definitions and conceptions of evaluation, many administrators use evaluation funds for activities that are more appropriately classified as research, on the one hand, or program management, on the other.

Labor's Establishment

Labor is a smaller department than HEW, with a narrower mission and a more compact evaluation establishment. But that does not necessarily render its evaluation activities orderly or coherent. There are intricacies in DOL too that muddle the way evaluations are carried out and complicate the analysis of how evaluation fits into the process of policy development.

The DOL organizational structure for evaluation resembles that of HEW, but the smaller scale of operations and historical developments creates dramatically different conditions. The Office of the Assistant Secretary for Policy, Evaluation and Research (ASPER) is roughly analagous to the HEW Office of the Assistant Secretary for Planning and Evaluation, albeit with significant differences in substance and style. In theory, ASPER is responsible for internal housekeeping duties, as well as its own evaluation agenda. The former responsibility is intended to provide technical assistance and review evaluation activities, while the latter has involved investigating broad policy areas that cut across departmental lines or go beyond the program concerns of the Employment and Training Administration (ETA). In practice, ASPER has, at times, exercised a heavy hand in shaping the evaluation activities throughout the department, pursuing an evaluation agenda based on limited operational knowledge which has sometimes been completely inappropriate and even damaging to program implementation.

Five operational programs in Labor have formal evaluation offices, but only the Office of Program Evaluation and Research in the Employment and Training Administration is sufficiently developed to make policy contributions. Excluding the temporary demonstration projects mandated by the Youth Employment and Demonstration Projects Act, the lion's share of evaluation is undertaken by the ETA Office of Policy, Evaluation and Research. ETA accounts for most of the dollars allocated to the entire department, and spends a commensurate proportion of all departmental evaluation and research funds.

THE TURF FACTOR

Among the competing interests that vie for program resources and administrators' time, evaluation normally gets a low priority. Given the choice, most administrators would probably pare it down to eliminate a source of aggravation and augment program operations. But they do not have much choice. Legislative mandates and top policy decisions frequently override managers' preferences. Occasionally, demands by the news media or groups interested in the performance of a specific program can also be irresistible.

At HEW there is an unwritten doctrine of agency sovereignty in program evaluation, a reflection of the federal system where each bureau chief controls his or her own fiefdom. Given the countless missions of HEW, it is assumed that each agency head generally knows best. The Assistant Secretary for Planning and Evaluation usually offers technical assistance only when asked. Although that office reviews all agency plans, including some invitations to prospective evaluators, most agency evaluation proceeds with remarkable independence. Substantial evaluation funds are available at the disposal of the assistant secretary for financing evaluations without interfering with agency plans. It is also not likely that the assistant secretary has the power to intrude on agency policy. But some of the independence that agency evaluators enjoy is due to a belief in the assistant secretary's office that little is to be gained—intellectually, politically, or programmatically—from a more centralized system.

The decentralization of HEW evaluation may be the best arrangement for that department, but it certainly involves costs. Quality control suffers, and could be improved by a more vigorous central review. Some agency work also appears to be parochial and self-serving. While in existence as a separate agency, the Social and Rehabilitation Service conducted successive evaluations of vocational rehabilitation programs. Relying upon questionable methodological designs, most concluded that these programs were very effective in making their clients employable. The National Institute of Education has repeatedly been attacked by congressional critics for abstruse studies having little bearing on important policy issues. In a fit of pique, the Senate Appropriations Committee went so far as to eliminate the Institute's entire budget for fiscal year 1977. Although the funds were later restored, the basic criticism still held. The Institute's evaluation work was independent from the Office of Education and largely divorced from the latter's operational responsibilities because HEW lacked the machinery to exercise constraints.

No such claims of agency sovereignty could be made in the Department of Labor. In recent years, evaluators' activities at the assistant secretary level have been overbearing in contrast to the limited power exercised by their HEW counterparts. Political considerations may account for some of the differences. HEW agencies have their own constituencies to support and defend them. The Social Security Administration, Office of Education and National Institute of Health all operate under legislation that gives their heads statutory power independent of the secretary. The legacy of HEW's creation—an afterthought consolidating a number of previously existing agencies—is a chain of command that does not always give the secretary the final say. In contrast, the Department of Labor preceded the establishment of its component agencies with the exception of the Bureau of Labor Statistics. Agency heads have not enjoyed the statutory autonomy of their HEW counterparts, and many of the programs—young and still evolving—have not developed strong outside constituencies.

In keeping with the strong central control in DOL, the central evaluation agency in the department has gained a tight grip over all the department's research and evaluation. What is now the Office of the Assistant Secretary for Policy, Evaluation and Research was established in 1963 "to anticipate changes that would affect wage earners, and to develop policies and programs to promote their welfare in the context of such developments."[5] Focusing initially on policy studies and planning, ASPER virtually ignored serious evaluation efforts. Whatever evaluation was undertaken in the department was located in what is now the Employment and Training Administration.

In the several years that followed, ASPER stayed out of the mainstream of policy development. Then, in the early Nixon administration, it sought to enhance its participation in departmental policy formulation and evaluation. But the Manpower Administration could not be easily dislodged from its preeminent role. It had the funds and the troops to rebuff any onslaughts from ASPER. In the early 1970s, ASPER was briefly influential, having hired some qualified evaluation staff, and its

5. "History of ASPER: 1969-1976," Office of the Assistant Secretary for Policy, Evaluation and Research, U.S. Department of Labor, Washington, January 1977, p. 1.

top officials had the ears of the department's policymakers who identified critical policy issues that needed evaluating. ASPER also provided some very effective direction to evaluation activities throughout the department to assure their responsiveness to the needs of departmental heads and to use evaluation findings for policy development. However, this era was short-lived.

The frequent changes of secretaries in the early 1970s upset the delicate relationship that had given ASPER its power. While its technical competence remained intact, its influence waned. Its senior officials were rebuffed and disregarded by a succession of secretaries and ASPER lost most of its effectiveness in leading the department's evaluation activities and in directing its own evaluation to relevant policy questions. Through the mid-1970s, its evaluation guidance was marked increasingly by a slavish devotion to methodological rigor and an absence of policy relevance. Cut off from the principal policymakers, it imposed itself on the rest of the evaluation establishment as an uninvited meddling model manipulator. In the late 1970s, however, stability in the office of the assistant secretary, better access to top policymakers in DOL, and a willingness on the part of those policymakers to pay attention to ASPER all appear to be improving its impact.

ASPER's influence over agency evaluation begins with the planning process. Although it has a review function much like that of the HEW Office of the Assistant Secretary for Planning and Evaluation, this is a pro forma exercise because of its prior involvement in the formulation of evaluation plans. ASPER personnel participate in the planning process by identifying topics for study and dictating the methodologies. Where agency evaluation plans do not address the issues that ASPER considers to be important, or where their methodologies are not suitably sophisticated (regardless of the reasons), ASPER steps in with its own ideas. In budgeting agency evaluation activities, ASPER holds the purse strings and also has considerable influence over agency thinking. In 1975, research and development committees were set up in each program area to institutionalize previously informal communications between evaluators and administrators.

The purpose of these committees is to pick up where evaluation planning leaves off, maintaining a sense of rapport between program people and evaluators during the conduct of evaluation. Although the groups do not always contribute appreciably to the success of evaluation projects, ASPER is always involved and uses the opportunity to bring its opinions to bear.

In the role that it has carved out, ASPER is not just an adjunct to evaluation planning and management, but serves as another administrative layer superimposed on agency evaluators. It duplicates their responsibilities in a way that often pits ASPER opinions directly against agency thinking, creating what may be, in many cases, an unnecessary tension between departmental and program level interests without the benefit of a complementary management process to resolve them.

In the case of the fledgling Occupational Safety and Health Administration (OSHA), ASPER was up to its usual form. In OSHA's first few years of existence, there was confusion about the agency's mission, to say nothing about a lack of evaluation expertise and mistrust of the role of evaluation. ASPER took what amounted to an adversary role, and further contributed to OSHA's difficulties by evaluating its activities with little regard to legislative mandates or stated agency objectives. Program performance was roundly criticized from all quarters and evaluation was seen by some as one more opening for criticism. Consequently, little attention was given to evaluation within OSHA and any attempts to impose it from the outside were viewed with suspicion.

Not surprisingly, agency evaluators in the past have not entirely appreciated the intrusion of ASPER's housekeeping activities either. In many cases, its technical assistance is seen as interference. ASPER's original role was to make the final review of evaluation plans. However, because ASPER perceives the agencies' in-house capabilities as being limited, it has often been involved at every stage of evaluation management from preliminary planning to final product review (agency evaluators see this nitpicking attention to details best handled by them). ASPER's attempted involvement has been encouraged by the weakness of agency evaluation staff. But the factors that inhibit evaluation by agency staff have also inhibited ASPER's efforts. To overcome these methodological and substantive obstacles requires not regimentation but a thorough understanding of agency missions and need for knowledge.

In the past, agency evaluators have not regarded their limited staff size and capabilities as adequate justification for ASPER's activism, which they have seen as an unwelcome intrusion of abstract thinking into a pragmatic environment. ASPER's independent attempts to evaluate departmental programs have been seen as well-intentioned but inappropriate. Whereas ASPER staff have believed that agency evaluators embrace outmoded and inferior methodologies and approaches, many program evaluators and managers have thought that ASPER was—to borrow the late Jacob Viner's apt phrase—building models without vital organs, that is, models with little relevance to agency needs. Early in its existence, the Occupational Safety and Health Administration, charged with regulating workplace safety and health conditions, had disagreements with ASPER about evaluating the economic impact of regulatory actions. OSHA had prepared inflationary impact statements based on the cost of compliance to assess how to phase in enforcement of its regulations most economically. ASPER prepared cost-benefit analyses based on assigning dollar values to benefits of the lives saved and injuries prevented and the costs of controlling occupational health hazards. These analyses were used in selectively applying regulations where benefits exceeded costs. OSHA, which had to clear its impact statements through ASPER, disagreed with the latter's approach on a number of grounds. In a report that accompanied his resignation, one former assistant secretary for OSHA stated that ". . . the methodology associated with such [cost-benefit] analyses is in its formative stages. The variance placed on any estimates of dollar benefits of disease and death is so great as to be virtually useless." He further criticized ASPER for opposing the spirit of the law, which required the uniform application of regulations.[6] In short,

---

6. Morton Corn, "Status Report on OSHA," submitted to the Secretary of Labor, January 12, 1977, pp. 29-30.

an operating agency criticized ASPER for applying a methodology that was unrelated to its real policy choices.

Another criticism leveled against ASPER has been that its staff are too far removed from program operations to be sensitive to their problems. Evaluations favored by ASPER have tended to examine micro- or macroeconomic issues, relying heavily on assumptions but little on actual program experience. In contrast, agency evaluations address narrower and more practical programmatic issues. Many resemble process evaluations, assessing the results rather than basic underlying premises of program strategies. In 1974, the Manpower Administration completed an evaluation of the public employment program; the following year, ASPER completed a related evaluation of public service employment programs. The former focused on the effect of the program in job creation/job restructuring, characteristics of the workforce, and changes in municipal services. The latter also examined the effects of public service jobs on the composition of municipal labor forces, but went further. Indulging in simulations (read guesses) to estimate the impact of the public service program, it tried to analyze more fundamental economic issues such as how public service jobs affect local labor markets, behavior of labor, and aggregate levels of employment. The results were publicized as Department of Labor findings, although the conclusions were based more on the ideologies of the evaluators than on facts.[7] A 1976 study by the Employment and Training Administration examined the effectiveness of the Work Incentive Program in placing AFDC recipients in permanent jobs and improving their chances of becoming economically self-sufficient. In contrast, a 1974 report by ASPER concentrated on the macroeconomic issues of net increases in aggregate output,

---

7. J. A. Reyes Associates, Inc., "The Public Employment Program: An Impact Assessment," Department of Labor, Manpower Administration Contract Number 63-1173-03, August 31, 1974; and George Johnson and James D. Tomola, "The Efficacy of Public Service Employment Programs," (revised) Technical Analysis Paper #17A, Office of Evaluation, Office of the Assistant Secretary for Policy, Evaluation and Research, Department of Labor, June 1975.

income distribution effects of WIN, and the trend of aggregate AFDC costs over time.[8]

In short, the ASPER evaluations tended to speculate about broad policy issues, filling the gaps in programmatic data with heroic assumptions. But there was little appreciation in ASPER's work for the reality of program operations and the manner in which they impinge on policy. The style reflected the fact that ASPER evaluators were more removed from decisionmakers than were agency evaluators. Hence its criteria for judging program performance differed and its results conflicted with those of the operating agency. The tension this created was natural and predictable. While agency staff felt somewhat threatened, ASPER staff justified it as a natural process for airing all sides of an issue. The ASPER standards for performance were not necessarily undertaken as attempts to second-guess agency sponsored evaluations; rather they were merely seen as alternative perspectives. But the reality and expectations they implied were misleading and, rather than presenting the clarification of another legitimate view, served to confuse. Few policymakers or news media personnel could realistically evaluate the heroic assumptions of model builders and their often spurious exercises were too often mistaken for rigorous analysis. The net effect of ASPER's rambunctiousness was to alienate many program managers and reduce ASPER's ability to lead credible evaluation activities in the department.

Despite many attempts, ASPER was not able to reestablish itself as a serious policy analysis arm of the Labor Secretary until 1977. Then continuity in personnel, good rapport between the offices of the secretary and the assistant secretary, and marked improvement in ASPER's ability to direct impact evaluations began to bring ASPER back into the mainstream of serious program evaluation and policy analysis. However, much of this progress has been interrupted by pressures to respond to outside

8. Pacific Training and Technical Assistance Corporation, "Comprehensive Methodological Issues and Some Initial Results," Technical Analysis Paper #15, Office of the Assistant Secretary for Policy, Evaluation and Research, Department of Labor, February 1974.

priorities. Prodded by the White House to tackle such issues as comprehensive employment and training legislation and welfare reform, ASPER has had to neglect some narrower, but nevertheless important, departmental policy concerns.

MANAGING EVALUATION

The quality of management—of selecting, grooming, and monitoring contractors and consultants—is crucial to the success of evaluation projects. In the executive branch, very little evaluation is done in-house. Nearly all is done under grant or contract.

At HEW (excluding the Social Security Administration), in-house projects account for no more than 5 percent of all evaluations and of all set-aside expenditures. In addition, outside projects are more readily identifiable than in-house evaluation, which is often indistinguishable from routine management review and analysis.

However, some clearly identifiable evaluation activities are conducted in-house. The utilization of evaluation findings for administrative and policy purposes is an important in-house activity, although it commands only modest resources. In this utilization process, contract reports are only an intermediary product or raw material. For example, practically every evaluation effort in the Office of Education (OE) collects data from state and local education offices and institutions. If the information needed is not part of an ongoing record file, OE contracts for its collection, perhaps after some statistical tests to assure proper sampling and an optimal organization of the data. OE then uses the contractor's product for analysis to answer the primary evaluation questions. Similarly, the Social Security Administration contracts most of its field survey work and then analyzes the data in-house. Once evaluations have been completed, most agencies prepare "policy implication papers" (PIPs) and executive summaries of the findings.

At the Department of Labor, a much larger proportion of evaluation work is done in-house. As late as 1975, in-house efforts accounted for about a fifth of all evaluations.[9] In keeping with its academic aura, most of ASPER's in-house studies had involved investigation of specialized methodological issues of doubtful policy significance. The result did little more than add another layer of obfuscation and belabored technical detail. The analyses responded less to specific needs than to the aspirations of ASPER analysts to advance their academic standing.

In contrast, the evaluations of the Employment and Training Administration and its predecessor, the Manpower Administration, have reflected operational needs, and the in-house staff studies have, for the most part, aimed at program management problems. The advantage that the in-house evaluations presumably enjoy is that, because they are not made public, they encourage more candor on the part of program officials. While probably little of substance in the uncirculated reports is lost to the world because of this emphasis on management issues, the practice fosters a kind of dualism in which managers respond differently to in-house and to contract evaluators.

Some officials and outside observers would prefer more in-house evaluation in the executive branch, arguing that the insights, cooperation, and continuity that can be achieved with in-house staff are vital if evaluation is to be more than a pro forma exercise. The logic of these arguments notwithstanding, there are extremely strong forces limiting the amount of in-house work being done now, and there is not likely to be much more of it in the near future. All executive agencies operate under personnel ceilings that hold their employment to congressionally-determined levels. An increase in evaluation personnel would require a decrease somewhere else, robbing Peter to pay Paul. Given the relatively low priority accorded to evaluation work, such increases in evaluation personnel are unlikely. However, in spite of the ceilings on personnel, creating the illusion that the size of the

---

9. "Program Evaluation Studies in the U.S. Department of Labor," Office of the Assistant Secretary for Policy, Evaluation and Research, U.S. Department of Labor, July 1975.

federal payroll is kept under strict controls, the funds available for evaluation are relatively generous. These funds are frequently used to hire contractors, consultants, or persons on loan from other agencies and institutions who are not reckoned against agency personnel ceilings. Hence, the full-time equivalent of evaluation personnel supported by HEW and Labor under contract and consultant arrangements far exceeds the number who are employed in-house. One labor-sponsored study found 58 consulting firms doing business with Labor and HEW along a six block stretch of downtown Washington.[10]

Staff shortages may also place constraints on the number and quality of contracts. Despite the extensive use of contracts, the Public Health Service has been able to spend only a third of its set-aside funds because it has lacked the staff to develop requests for proposals, review bids, monitor contractors or review completed evaluations. If other HEW agencies spend more of their set-asides, that is partly because they give less attention than Public Health Service to overseeing contracts. Most evaluation staff agree that some contract work is off target, incomplete, or otherwise unsatisfactory because staff resources have been stretched too thin. While it would take only a few additional staff to improve HEW's contract monitoring, it would take a large number—several hundred—to conduct all evaluations in-house. And, by contracting, HEW can choose from a larger pool of talent than it could hire directly.

At DOL, in-house staff have not been stretched so thinly. As the number of personnel has declined, contract resources have also declined or grown only slowly. The sole exception has been in the Office of Youth Programs, which is benefiting from a massive infusion of resources for evaluation, research and demonstration, in connection with demonstration legislation enacted in 1977. Except for that office, evaluation budgets have not grown in proportion to aggregate agency budgets, as none of Labor's agencies operates under set-asides. Management is also simpler,

---

10. Albert D. Biderman and Laure M. Sharp, *The Competitive Evaluation Research Industry* (Washington: Bureau of Social Science Research, Inc., 1972), p. 33.

being controlled by a centralized office rather than dispersed among many programs. As programs have been added, evaluation functions have been grafted on to existing organizations, lending more continuity and coherence to evaluation policies. The ability to conduct a sizeable in-house study program indicates a better balance than HEW enjoys.

But staff limitations are not the only reason for conducting evaluation by contract. It is presumed that because of persuasive influences within agencies, agency personnel evaluating their own program have a hard time being objective, and an even harder time achieving credibility for their studies. This has been the underlying assumption that has been so instrumental in keeping contractors in business.[11] Less attention has been paid to the putative objectivity of contractors whose interest it is to please their sponsors. A survey of social policy experts done for the Research and Technical Programs Subcommittee of the House Committee on Government Operations lent support for this rationale as far back as the mid-1960s. One observer stated:

> I do not think that federal agencies should *themselves* conduct *any* kind of social research. My reason is that the value of any kind of social research is greatly influenced by the amount of autonomy of the researcher. I think that it is very easy for intra-agency social research to become a political and policy football.[12]

Unfortunately, relying on outside talent for an evaluation does not automatically guarantee independent work that will be free of agency biases. Not wishing to be killed for bearing ill tidings, the hired evaluator who depends on getting evaluation contracts or grants from an agency may be less than candid about program shortcomings.

---

11. Harold Orlans, *Contracting for Knowledge* (San Francisco: Jossey-Bass, 1973), pp. 134-35.

12. Alvin W. Gouldner, in *The Use of Social Research in Federal Domestic Programs,* U.S. House of Representatives, Research and Technical Programs Subcommittee of the Committee on Government Operations (Washington: Government Printing Office, 1967), Part III, pp. 102-103.

But disregarding for a moment the relative merits of outside and in-house performers, there is a singular virtue to setting aside a pot of money for outside evaluation instead of using the money for in-house personnel. Administrators tend to downplay the significance of evaluation, and when it is not specifically provided for in legislation and must be done by in-house personnel, it can be too easily pushed aside by higher priorities.

One alternative approach adopted by Labor to overcome personnel ceiling constraints and at the same time assure the availability of evaluation assistance is to establish nonprofit organizations that couple evaluation with program administration chores. Largely financed by federal funds, but with some seed and "mad" money provided by foundations to assure a degree of independence, these organizations conduct research, demonstrations, and evaluations. The Manpower Demonstration Research Corporation is possibly the most prominent of the "intermediaries." The 1977 youth legislation requiring massive research and evaluation spawned Youthwork and the Corporation for Youth Enterprises. There are many ways to skin a cat, and government officials are learning the skills needed to survive and to carry out their functions.

OUTSIDE EVALUATION

Since fiscal 1974, most HEW sponsored evaluations have been done under contract. Before restrictions were introduced in 1974, HEW obtained much of its outside evaluation by grant. The latter device had its advantages for both program administrators who still had a lot to learn and hustling grantees who had a lot to earn. As the Great Society programs got underway in the 1960s, program administrators realized the gaps in their knowledge for dealing with the new challenges, and the grantees were only too happy to make an effort to find answers to uncertain questions. The response was a move to evaluate programs and support research activities furthering understanding of social problems and the options for alleviating them. Grants were a logical way to attain the objectives. They were open-ended and left the grantee with a pot of money, free to investigate whatever issues were considered important. If program administrators did not know what questions to ask, they left it to the grantee to figure out the line of inquiry. The results were predictable. Some of the grants yielded relevant findings; others contributed to a more general body of knowledge. Many efforts turned out to be nothing more than fishing expeditions or, more frequently, examinations of issues which interested the investigators (who often proposed the projects in the first place). They were off target, slow in coming, and of little use to decisionmakers. They did little more than satisfy the curiosity investigators had about their own pet topics and raise their living standards.

In 1974, as part of a movement to require competitive bidding, HEW virtually ruled out any further support of evaluations with grants. Part of the rationale was that effective program evaluation demanded assurances of more agency control and decision relevance than provided by grants. They were deemed inadequate vehicles for obtaining timely and useful information and answers to specified questions. But there were other motives as well. Many political appointees of the Nixon and Ford administrations were uncomfortable with the evaluators who had been the beneficiaries of the grant system and with the policy implications of some of their work. The hope was that contracts would inject an entrepreneurial spirit into the evaluation establishment, encourage competition, and attract pragmatic investigators whose message would be more to the liking of agency policymakers having greater control in selecting issues for evaluation. Another reason behind the push for competitive contracting was the notion that evaluation could be treated as a commodity and that there was a market for evaluation services that functioned reasonably well. Both assumptions have remained unproven but nonetheless inviolable.

Today, grants are still used extensively for research and selected demonstration projects having built-in evaluation component requirements. However, contracts are now preferred for evaluation projects.

In DOL, no formal department edict has proscribed evaluation by grant, but a long-standing policy favors the use of contracts over grants. The glib assertion is that grants are used when it does not matter what happens to the money. While that understates the obligation that grantees have to the department, contracts do impose performance obligations that are unrealistic for grants. For this reason, contracts are used almost exclusively in the evaluation work where the agency can specify what it is seeking, while grants are made to academic institutions and for efforts supporting a specific researcher when few funds are involved.

In sum, evaluations have been viewed as necessary to provide specific information needs, and contracts have given both HEW and Labor greater control over deadlines and the course of research. But they have not eliminated substantive problems of evaluation, such as the ability to raise the right questions, to provide guidance, or to evoke and sustain the best efforts of investigators.

To Compete or Not to Compete

Agency staff may use either noncompetitive or competitive "Requests-for-Proposal" (RFP) contracts. In noncompetitive or, as it is often called, sole-source procurement, an agency selects an evaluator without going through an open bidding process that brings other contractors into consideration. The recipient of a sole-source contract is obligated to provide an agreed-upon and specified product or service.

Sole-source awards account for some 60 percent of all federal contracts and grants. The justifications for this type of procurement are that a particular evaluation calls for unique capabilities, and that the contracting agency knows who the best performer is. The unique qualifications may include the fact that the contractor may have the acknowledged experts in a field, proprietary rights to necessary information, or distinctive prior experience. Whatever the precise reason, the presumption is that no one else can do the job as well or as promptly for the same price or at any reasonable price.

Sole-source contracting has other important advantages. It is usually faster than a competitive process. Despite the extra justification it entails, it can usually save two or three months and frequently more by eliminating the preparation of a request for proposals, advertising, and reviewing proposals. Sole-source awards also encourage closer relationships between evaluators and agency officials. They indicate a personal or intellectual compatibility and trust between the agency officials and the contractor. Sole-source evaluators tend to be repeaters much more often than competitive award evaluators. The continuity reduces the time an evaluator needs to become familiar with agency procedure and facilitates the flow of information. Under these conditions evaluations are often better adapted to agency needs. By relying upon recognized expertise, sole-source procurement tends to put more emphasis on the finished product as contrasted with the RFP route where agency officials are obliged to assign staff for preparation of proposals.

Of course, noncompetitive procurement is subject to abuse when the healthy rapport turns into a cozy relationship between officials and evaluators. Evaluators quickly learn the party line that officials want to hear. Agencies may find themselves paying more for sycophancy and getting less information than they would in an open market. Because of the potential for abuse, sole-source procurements are governed by special regulations.

Both HEW and DOL require extensive documentation to justify all sole-source awards. Cumbersome review procedures control the award of any contract in excess of $25,000. The process may reduce favoritism, but it introduces delays and red tape. This frequently discourages resort to sole-source and, as a result, the award may go to the applicant who has the resources to cope with the obstacles rather than to do the most qualified job. Not surprisingly, the General Accounting Office and Congress view sole-source awards as smacking of cronyism and favor the tight control of the practice. The Nixon and Ford administrations favored competitive bidding because of ideological convictions and a suspicion of the social scientists who have tended to receive noncompetitive awards. The Carter administration has also sought to reduce sole-source awards. Accordingly, contracts for evaluations have generally been declining in number and size. Since the line between research and evaluation is frequently blurred, it is difficult to quantify the number of sole-source awards that might be classified as dealing with evaluation. But one count shows that in fiscal 1971, the Office of the Assistant Secretary for Planning and Evaluation in HEW awarded 65 percent of its contracts and 57 percent of its funds in sole-source form. Two years later the ratio of noncompetitive contracts declined to about a third of the total funds, along with a decline in the number of contracts.[13] By 1978, officials estimated that less than 10 percent of HEW evaluation funds were awarded noncompetitively.

At Labor, sole-source procurements for research have not met a similar fate. The Office of Policy, Evaluation and Research prefers sole-source to competitive contracts for the same reasons that it prefers grants to contracts. Its strongest argument is that to procure research by competitive contract is to treat the buying of knowledge and insights on the same basis as the procurement of a tank or a typewriter. Unlike hardware procurements, research reports are highly individualized—the products of distinctive craftsmen and professionals that defy advance specifications. Moreover, if research awarded were funded exclusively by contracts resulting from a competitive process, many academic scholars would avoid the employment and training arena. Competition forces research into a production mode that rewards the grantsmanship capability of the more experienced consultant organizations and crowds the academics out of the market. Sole-source contracts also help research managers keep in close contact with the academic world and arrange quickly for special studies that may be needed.

Labor's Assistant Secretary for Policy, Evaluation and Research consistently relies almost exclusively on sole-source contractors for evaluations. As ASPER does not award grants for research, sole-source contracts serve as an effective substitute.

---

13. *Departments of Labor and Health, Education, and Welfare Appropriations for 1977,* Appropriations Committee, U.S. House of Representatives, 94th Congress, 2nd Session (Washington: Government Printing Office, 1976), p. 936, and committee files.

At HEW, the Social Security Administration's Office of Research and Statistics (ORS) has done a great deal of sole-source contracting in the past. Unlike other HEW evaluation units, ORS is heavily involved in basic research as well as program evaluation. It also does a great deal of in-house work. By one estimate, slightly more than half of all the ORS contracts and contract expenditures in 1975 and 1976 were sole-source. However, by 1978, ORS was succumbing to departmental directives and awarded none of its contracts on that basis.

The competitive award process hinges on the request for proposals (RFP) or bids from prospective contractors. RFPs are prepared by agency evaluation staff with assistance from program personnel and agency administrators. As an extension of the evaluation planning process, agency staff may specify the objectives of the project, the methodology and sampling specifications, allowable statistical margins of error, and general format requirements. The RFP poses the questions to be answered and the "specs" or conditions that must be met, so that potential bidders can determine whether they should enter the competition. If they decide to compete, the RFP serves as a guide for their proposed work plan and budget.

RFPs can play an important role in shaping the nature and quality of the evaluation product, indicating the approach that is required and the time allotted for completion of the project. Unfortunately, many RFPs fail to do so. Although the General Accounting Office has yet to issue a report on the preparation of RFPs by agency personnel, individual GAO investigators have found it often to be a case of the contractor tail wagging the agency dog. Too often the RFP lists broad requirements applicable to any evaluation, without specifying the methodology, objectives and data that are sought in a given project. In these cases, the contractors must add flesh to the skeleton and determine the approach they will take on technical issues and even, at times, define the issues. Although they are not in the position to determine the policies and programs to be evaluated, they often determine the relevance of evaluation findings.

Once the request for proposal has been prepared, an open competition may ensue in which any contractor is free to submit bids; alternately, a more restricted procedure of negotiations with selected contractors may be employed. Open competition is preferred by the General Accounting Office and contract officers more often than by evaluation officers. But, it is slow, costly, and does not always assure that the best product will be obtained.

In open competition, the availability of an RFP is announced in the *Commerce Business Daily,* a government publication for advertising federal competitive procurements. In a number of cases, agencies take the pains to mail RFPs directly to qualified contractors to assure that they are notified of the competition. Contractors who choose to compete submit proposals and bids. The bids are then reviewed by a committee of project officers, program personnel, and contract officers, and an award is negotiated with the contractor who is ranked first on a composite score in which points are assigned for such factors as cost, methodologies, the qualifications of staff, and prior experience and performance.

Notwithstanding its attractiveness, open competition has its costs. Being open, the process is, on the surface, very egalitarian. But this requires the agency to undertake the effort and expense of mailing RFPs to many contractors who are only remotely interested in bidding. After bids are submitted, the agency must mount an intensive effort to weed out the unqualified bidders. One study of competitive procurements found that 13 open solicitations yielded more than 2,500 requests for RFPs and netted 286 bids. The RFP mailing, responding to inquiries, and the subsequent review process required a massive effort by the contracting agencies.[14]

In addition to the direct expense to the agency in open competition, the cumulative expense to contractors can be staggering. The Bureau of Social Science Research reviewed 444 proposals submitted for 12 awards valued at $4 million. Interviews

---

14. Albert D. Biderman and Laure M. Sharp, *An Analysis of 36 Competitive Procurements of Social Program Evaluation Studies* (Washington: Bureau of Social Science Research, Inc., 1974), p. 11.

at fifteen firms submitting bids established that the cost of proposal preparation ranged from $200 to $16,000, with a median of $3,000. The authors estimated that it cost contractors more than $1.3 million to bid for $4 million worth of contracts.[15]

Following classical economic doctrine, supporters of open competition assert that the high cost of incompetence drives unproductive and inferior contractors out of the market. However, if it assures a higher quality of contractor in the long run, it is only at high overhead cost to the survivors. Furthermore, that analysis, as well as the entire RFP mechanism, is based on the heroic assumption that RFP quality correlates well with the quality of evaluation products. As a consequence, it appears that an inordinate amount of the "expertise" purchased actually goes into preparing the RFP.[16] In actuality, the system of open competition puts a premium on proposal preparation, not project performance.

Agencies sometimes expedite procurement by distributing an RFP to a restricted number of organizations rather than advertising it for open competition. The distribution may be based on reputation or on prior contract or grant work with the agency. The attempt is to foster a degree of competition sufficient to make a good choice but not wasteful in time and money. The restricted competition approach signifies that the agency is seriously interested in proposals from designated contractors. It improves the response to RFPs and nets a higher proportion of good proposals. However, it also leaves agency officials open to challenge from organizations that were left out and may result in delaying the award of a contract.

Preselection practices vary. In one case, the National Institute of Education combined fifteen evaluation proposals and then mailed the package to 447 preselected bidders. Usually, however, preselection is more restricted. The median number of bids invited in one survey of evaluation contract offerings was 13. The survey

---

15. Biderman and Sharp, *The Competitive Evaluation Research Industry*, pp. 38-39.

16. Albert D. Biderman and Laure M. Sharp, "The Evaluation Research Community: RFP Readers, Bidders, and Winners," *Evaluation*, Vol. 2, No. 1, 1974, pp. 36-40.

showed that, when open competition was employed, one in nine organizations that asked for an RFP submitted a proposal, whereas with preselection, nearly half of the organizations responded.[17]

THE PERFORMERS

Because the executive branch does so little social program evaluation and research in-house, the qualifications and selection of performers are vital to the federal evaluation effort. What performer characteristics are important in influencing the overall quality of the work? The question has no easy answers. Different conditions and circumstances call for different strengths in evaluators. Even when a precise set of qualifications is needed, it is not always clear which organizations can best supply them.

The research and evaluation community is often dichotomized into for-profit and nonprofit sectors. For-profit organizations are commercial ventures organized to make money. They are frequently viewed as hired guns, ready to evaluate anything for anyone under any terms and conditions, so long as they make a profit.[18] The nonprofit organizations, either affiliated with academic institutions or independent entities, are supposedly more mission oriented than for-profit firms, concentrating on specific policy areas, disciplines, or methods. In fact, many compete in as wide a range of areas as any for-profit group.

Clearly, this dichotomy is misleading. The real distinctions between the two kinds of organizations are more obvious to an accountant or tax lawyer than to an agency evaluator looking for a conscientious performer. Many nonprofit organizations are just as promotional as the most spirited for-profit firms. Although they are tax sheltered, theoretically serving educational and scientific purposes, they are in fact often in the thick of competition, vying with one another and with for-profit firms for the same work.

17. Biderman and Sharp, *An Analysis of 36 Competitive Procurements of Social Program Evaluation Studies,* pp. 23-24 and 46-47.

18. Ilene N. Bernstein and Howard E. Freeman, *Academic and Entrepreneurial Research* (New York: Russell Sage Foundation, 1975), pp. 56-63.

Many are in the midst of an identity crisis over everything except whether to retain their tax exemption, and some have relinquished that status.[19] Some observers see no difference between them and for-profits: "In many cases the so-called nonprofit organization is in fact profit making in every sense of the word with the exception of tax status."[20] The frequent movement of staff among contracting organizations and the use of consultantships, subcontracts, and joint bids to bind organizations together further blur distinctions among the different kinds of institutions. For example, academics, the group whose contributions presumably make the work of nonprofit and academic institutions more "rigorous," frequently serve as consultants to for-profit firms and nonprofit institutes. From the standpoint of agency administrators, the profit/nonprofit categorization is of little value in determining who should do a particular evaluation.

Another tempting way to categorize performers is according to the academic qualifications of their staff. However, there is little demonstrated relation between the quality of an organization's performance and the numbers and kinds of degrees its staff have.[21] As in the case of teaching, degrees are far from perfect proxies for the substantive performance criteria.

JUDGING THE EVALUATORS

Because of the variety of conflicting demands placed upon evaluators, the task of determining who performs best cannot be undertaken uniformly and never with a great deal of confidence. Government evaluation is constantly caught in the tension between the demands for thoroughness and timeliness, for scientific rigor and policy relevance, for independence and familiarity, and between epistemological limits to what research can explain and the virtually unlimited numbers of questions

---

19. Orlans, pp. 137-138.

20. John H. Kofron, *The Use of Social Research in Federal Domestic Programs,* a staff study for the Committee on Government Operations, U.S. House of Representatives (Washington: Government Printing Office, April 1967), p. 112.

21. Bernstein and Freeman, pp. 99-134.

officials can reasonably and usefully raise. While the tensions do not always pull in exactly opposite directions, they constantly tear at work in process, diffusing its resources and objectives and often weakening its intellectual and practical impact. Because there is no single objective to government evaluations, no constant order of priority among its many objectives, and no valid and reliable way to differentiate among contractors, no one contractor or type of contractor is "best." Academic, nonprofit, and for-profit organizations each manifests a great range and variability in the quality of performance.

Methodological competence is often considered a strong point of academic evaluators. They are considered well qualified to conceptualize the goals of evaluation and to understand the theoretical underpinning of social programs and the forces that make them work or keep them from working.[22] But, methodological competence does not assure the usefulness of findings. This may not be a serious weakness in academic circles, but from the public policymaker's point of view, it is crucial. It is hard to justify a useless study.

Methodological adequacy is a necessary but insufficient condition for effective evaluation. For management and efficiency studies, sophisticated methodologies are often unnecessary.[23] While evaluation is more sophisticated today than in the early 1960s, it is not because of any profound conceptual progress. There have been no theoretical breakthroughs in understanding the social and intellectual problems which evaluations address. The breakthroughs have been strictly technical, primarily in the ability of computers to process and manipulate vast quantities of data. As one observer put it, "We've had an engineering advance but not a scientific advance."[24]

---

22. Bernstein and Freeman, pp. 83-98.

23. William A. Morrill and Walton J. Francis, "Evaluation from the HEW Perspective," remarks presented at the Federal Executive Institute Workshop on Program Management, May 3, 1976, p. 4.

24. Clark C. Abt, "The State of the Art of Program Evaluation," *Legislative Oversight and Program Evaluation,* proceedings of a seminar organized for the U.S. Senate Committee on Government Operations (Washington: Government Printing Office, May 1976), p. 314.

A performance criterion that sometimes conflicts with methodological adequacy is timeliness. How quickly can a performer conduct an evaluation; how well can he meet a deadline? How well can he balance the quality and timeliness of information? Greater certainty costs time and money. The collection, analysis, and presentation of added information raise costs and delay decisions. An accomplished performer must make many judicious compromises between the pressing demands for timeliness and for precise, reliable, and convincing information.

The demand for instant evaluations may jeopardize methodological adequacy by restricting the time for longitudinal studies or experimentation. It may serve to reduce sample sizes, to inhibit painstaking and meticulous procedures. The New Jersey Graduated Work Incentive experiment encountered just these kinds of problems when political pressures forced a premature presentation of findings. Most evaluations are subject to similar, although less dramatic, pressures.

There is no empirical evidence on the point, but profitmaking organizations claim to be the most dependable in meeting deadlines because that is their bread and butter. Academicians are presumably more loathe to cut methodological corners, because they are more interested in presenting a well-documented case than a quick and dirty analysis that relies on intuition and judgment as much as on hard, empirical data. Academia assigns greater value to careful, time-consuming research than to less careful, if more timely work. The payoff in the halls of academe in prestige and honor is for rigorous research which serves to advance a scholarly discipline rather than research meeting the practical needs of government. One analysis done as a follow-up to a congressional study reported that "among the kind of research singled out as inappropriate for universities were projects . . . providing quick answers. . . ."[25] Given the time pressures on many evaluation studies, it stands to reason that the academic role might be limited.

Social programs cannot be evaluated adequately by the concepts and methods of a single academic discipline. Neither the effects of

25. Orlans, p. 137.

the programs nor the problems they grapple with are unidimensional. There is more to unemployment than deficient aggregate demand or a mismatch between skills and available job openings. A variety of factors—political, sociological, psychological, historical, even medical and physical—also come into play. Welfare dependency is more than a sociological or psychological phenomenon; there are hard economic facts to consider. Housing problems are similarly the products of a constellation of interlocking forces. Because the problems are not one-dimensional, their adequate evaluation and resolution cannot be one-dimensional either. An ideal evaluation should conceptualize research and analyze all the interrelated aspects of a program and then design the elements of a new and better program. It should be rounded—or, in the parlance of the trade, the product should be a multidisciplinary intellectual enterprise. In practice, few evaluations achieve these goals and program administrators normally settle for less. There have been few renaissance men and women in the evaluation business.

For-profit organizations are fairly well staffed and organized to bring a breadth of expertise to bear on an evaluation project. They are not hindered by an academic (or governmental) structure that interferes with picking up (and dropping) specialized assistance fairly quickly. That gives commercial organizations flexibility. In contrast, academic organizations are likely to favor a narrow disciplinary approach. The basic cause of this rigidity that may pass for rigor is, again, the structure of academic rewards and incentives. There is a premium on specialization and pushing a particular discipline or subdiscipline to the limits. Academic departments, associations, and journals are similarly oriented. An evaluation of a social program that is methodologically sound, even if useless for policy formulation, is much more apt to be published in an academic journal than a more balanced assessment that examines several dimensions of the program's effectiveness which affect social and economic policy. This sovereign discipline mentality encourages a rigid approach to the academic study of social programs and contributes to the gap between conclusions that are conceptually sound and those that are politically and administratively feasible.

As a result, traditional academic performers are normally not held in high esteem by executive evaluation officers. Most prefer instead to do business with nonprofit and profitmaking organizations. Labor's ASPER, oriented more towards research than evaluation, has relied on academicians for evaluations. In some respects, its experience with them has left much to be desired, contributing to ASPER's difficulties. They have tended to force evaluations into narrow, fashionable, and artificial channels which oversimplify or ignore the major dimensions of programs lying outside their disciplinary blinders. More recently, ASPER has departed from the narrow and rigid evaluation emphasis, enhancing its effectiveness in the policy arena as a result.

Serious problems have also been encountered in the putative ability of academicians to extend the frontier of understanding of today's society and the government's roles in it. The highly specialized nature of evaluations and research makes it difficult to achieve a progressive improvement in our understanding of the effects of social programs. For example, sophisticated analyses of the factors affecting labor force participation go off on parallel lines that never intersect. And while the sociological or economic aspects of the problem may be explored in much detail, a unified explanation that might be useful in formulating comprehensive new policies eludes the analysts.

Searching for a middle ground between relatively superficial analyses of many profitmaking groups and the narrowness of academic work, some observers turn to research institutes housing specialists from different disciplines. The assumption is that by bringing diverse specialists together to concentrate on a particular policy area, both depth and breadth can be achieved. But, the assumption has been questioned.

> Interdisciplinary research . . . bears somewhat the same relation to the world of the mind as the idea of "man" or a global society bears to the world of nations: an ideal infrequently realized. Ralph Linton once remarked that the only genuinely interdisciplinary thinking took place when two disciplines were united in one mind. . . . But

> to assemble under one roof scholars from many
> disciplines does not necessarily bind their knowledge
> together any more firmly than separate papers are
> bound together in a book. Genuine intellectual
> integration of different disciplines remains rare, and the
> more disciplines that must be integrated, the rarer it is.[26]

Many close observers believe that the most important factor in a successful and influential evaluation is the evaluator's experience. Repeat performers know the standing of a program in a department and the Congress, the relative importance of different program services and constituencies, and the possible consequences of their findings. They are also familiar with agency personnel and the intricacies of bureaucratic politics, and their staying power may indicate a degree of commitment to certain policy areas. The success of repeaters may therefore also reflect their ability to consistently second-guess the biases of the proposal reviewers.

Assuring continuity in evaluations is problematical, though. For years, the HEW Office of the Assistant Secretary for Planning and Evaluation used sole-source contracting to achieve continuity in evaluation. The Office of Policy, Evaluation and Research in Labor's Employment and Training Administration still uses sole-source contracting, justifying it partly on the grounds that it contributes to a smoother accretion of knowledge. The Office of Evaluation manages to have a large volume of its evaluation work done by repeat performers. Contract bidding is certainly not "fixed;" the repeaters' success is based on their consistent submission of better proposals. Relatively few bidders compete for the office's small contracts—less than 40, on average, compared to over 100 that many HEW offices receive for each RFP. For important evaluations with more than one phase, or assessments of pilot programs, agencies sometimes negotiate sole-source contracts for later phases if the contractor does an adequate job on the first. Many educational and income maintenance evaluations have been conducted this way.

---

26. Orlans, p. 248.

It is hard to get a consensus among evaluators as to who can best institutionalize, or at least foster continuity. The argument that for-profit organizations are not the most suitable to sustain continuity may hold more true for small, struggling firms with high staff turnover than for large, more firmly established ones. But even where turnover is minimal, the same staff may not be continuously assigned to a long term project. Firms often use their most prominent staff to prepare proposals and then assign less experienced personnel to conduct the work. However, the same phenomenon occurs at universities and research institutes. To get their money's worth, knowledgeable evaluation officials focus on the personnel to be assigned to a specific study rather than on the overall reputation or "classification" of the organization.

THE INDEPENDENCE OF EVALUATORS

An important consideration in appraising and utilizing the findings of evaluation projects is the degree of independence of the evaluators. Some see this as the chief determinant of reliable evaluation—more significant than methodologies, credentials, or vantage point. The argument is that only an investigator with no vested interest in the findings can conduct a dispassionate inquiry and reach an objective conclusion.[27]

The credibility of an evaluation by an agency responsible for administering the program is a recurring theme in discussion of federal accountability. Congressional action on the Legislative Reorganization Act of 1970 and the Congressional Budget and Impoundment Control Act of 1974 reflected this concern. Congress wanted assessments by evaluators who were perceived to be objective and independent of program administrators. That wish underlay the new emphasis on program evaluation by the General Accounting Office. The feeling was that GAO analysts reporting directly to Congress would be more responsive to the needs of the Congress in carrying out its oversight functions. But the entrance of GAO into social program evaluation has not

---

27. Michael Scriven, "Evaluation Bias and Its Control," *Evaluation Studies Review Annual,* Gene V. Glass, editor (Beverly Hills, CA: Sage Publications, 1976), p. 120.

disposed of the objectivity issue. Even if GAO were technically equipped to undertake evaluations of social programs, it could not conduct all the evaluations that are needed by the Congress, let alone executive agencies.

Although in-house evaluation is not necessarily biased, it is not the most prudent policy to leave the fox to guard the hen house. With self evaluation, the appearance of objectivity is hard to sustain. Evaluators are subject to gross and subtle institutional and programmatic pressures. Daniel P. Moynihan stressed the difficult position of in-house evaluators, suggesting that objective evaluation of social programs is a contradiction in terms:

> The commitment to evaluation research is . . . fundamentally ambivalent; one of attraction and fear, trust and distrust. This is so not only because research of this kind can blow up in an administrator's face when it turns out his programs show little or none of the effects they are supposed to achieve, but more importantly, because in areas of social policy, facts are simply not neutral, however much we would hope to treat them as such. In social science data are political.[28]

Moreover, many agencies lack the necessary qualified staff. The logistics of conducting evaluation work with limited staff resources dictate that corners be cut. Sampling has to be restricted and heavy reliance must be placed on guidance and data provided by program operators, raising again the question of credibility. Moreover, experience so far with in-house evaluation shows that results are often not disclosed to the public. This may be justified when the study involves some of the finer points of management, but certainly not when it discloses major program failings.

In view of its obvious limitations, little in-house evaluation is conducted and the trend is to eliminate it altogether. Almost all HEW evaluation work and the majority of Labor's are conducted

---

28. Daniel P. Moynihan, "The Crisis of Confidence," in *The Use of Social Research in Federal Domestic Programs,* staff study prepared for the U.S. Congress, House of Representatives, Committee on Government Operations (Washington: Government Printing Office, April 1967), Part III, p. 581.

by outside contractors. Contracting for outside brains and hands does not eliminate conflicts of interest, but does put a certain distance between the person whose ox is being gored and the person whose ox is doing the goring. Debate focuses on which performers are most likely to be objective. Some argue that for-profit organizations are subservient to program administrators and whoever else butters their bread. They will lick and not bite the hand that feeds them. As one observer noted:

> [A] profit-making organization which either has a commercial interest in a particular product or conducts research for a firm with such an interest faces a conflict between the dispassionate pursuit of knowledge and the danger of uncovering truths harmful to that commercial interest; it is likely to concentrate its attention on profitable truths.[29]

But in this respect, too, the distinction between for-profit and nonprofit performers may be more illusory than real. All groups want a roof over their heads and money for groceries. The issue centers, therefore, on whether a performer wants an encore. Faculty do not depend on contracts, since their basic income derives from their teaching, though they benefit from them. Hence, they have a greater degree of independence from federal sponsors than the staff of organizations which subsist primarily on federal funds. But the price for the independence of faculty can be steep. Ad hoc investigators lack the familiarity with a program that continuing association produces and which is helpful or necessary to render an evaluation realistic and useful. Furthermore, professors are no less subject than the staff of private organizations to ideological biases and the conviction that one methodology or theory is consistently superior to another.

"Independence" and "objectivity"—"naivete" may be a more accurate word—bear costs: unfamiliarity with and insensitivity to program personnel, clientele, and operational conditions; uncertainty about contract performance; and ignorance of political and administrative realities. The more control govern-

---

29. Orlans, p. 140.

ment staff exercise to keep evaluations relevant, the less independent the evaluator will be. An evaluator with complete independence from the sponsor is also likely to be completely free of contractual obligations.

It is reasonable and proper to ask if the cost of much independence and objectivity is too high. A persuasive case can be made that the federal executive branch has shirked its direct responsibility for evaluation and wrongly allocated the staff at its disposal to less important duties. Granted an independent assessment of programs is necessary; but this does not absolve administrators from conducting their own assessments of the efforts that Congress entrusted to them.

Like everything else associated with evaluation, there are no simple solutions and certainly there is no single approach to the selection of performers for different kinds of evaluation. The minimal requirement of a good evaluator is a thorough understanding of the social programs and policies under study and the context in which they operate. No one can gain that kind of understanding except by personal involvement or close and continuous observation. The former condition calls for in-house evaluators; the latter, for private evaluators who have made a personal commitment to the subject.

5

Can Evaluation
Make a Difference?

Federal outlays surpassed the half trillion dollar mark in fiscal year 1979. Transfer payments alone accounted for nearly a sixth of all the disposable income available to the American people. Although this expansion of federal responsibilities has not been universally acclaimed, it is irrefutable that the government is becoming increasingly important in our daily lives. In a democracy, it is now more crucial than ever that the citizenry, not to mention the President, Congress, and public officials, be able to assess the impact of governmental activities. Rising concerns over government credibility make it especially important to establish appropriate means of finding out what the government's diverse missions are and how well it is accomplishing them, and that these findings be reported to the public.

Agency reports and press releases convey glowing, superficial, or soporific accounts of governmental operations, but rarely a candid, rounded, or realistic one. In the 1960s, the fashion was to proclaim that every new social effort was on mark and contributing to a better society. In the succeeding decade, excessive promises have been replaced by a pervasive negativism, with the usual pronouncement being that social programs have failed. President Jimmy Carter was elected on an anti-Washington platform, although once in office, he has followed the path of his

127

predecessors in supporting existing programs and adding some new ones. It is no surprise, therefore, that the public has been confused about the true impact of government social efforts.

In the private sector, a market test determines if a commodity or company is successful. According to conventional economics, the consumer is supreme. However, the market test measures only the costs and income of a company, not the nation. It effectively ignores real social costs that accrue to consumers and the public which are not reflected in market prices and production costs. For example, the price of a car does not include the costs of automobile accidents. Presumably, a safer car could be built, but at a much higher price to consumers. The market test has its flaws; but for the purposes for which it is intended, it is an incisive test of the quality of products and services.

That kind of test is not applicable to government programs. The closest possible approximation is whether Congress will "buy" a program and how much it will "pay" (appropriate) for it. If a program is refunded annually, it is viewed as a success. This version of the test is necessary but inadequate for determining the "success"—the social costs and benefits—of a government program. What is needed is a more rigorous test of merit and effectiveness. Congress rarely has adequate data to determine whether a given project or program is achieving its predetermined goals. Faced every year with the decision of whether to continue a program, Congress too often depends primarily upon past funding levels for setting future appropriations. Of course, Congress may also respond to the pressures of program supporters and critics. Objective analyses of what a program *does* and *does not* accomplish figure only marginally, if at all, in the decisions.

The limited use of evaluations in policymaking has been due in part to the dearth of definitive and pertinent assessments of government programs. Until recent years, this lack was not felt that strongly. As long as federal expenditures were rising, most social programs were virtually guaranteed continued, if not increased, appropriations. But those fat years may have ended, and there may no longer be something for everyone. Difficult decisions will have to be made. The new congressional budget process that forces expenditures to be considered in competition with one another, taxpayers' discontent, and the inflationary pressures generated by huge federal deficits have all focused policymakers' attention on the need for ranking and selecting programs which merit support and curtailing those that fall short of the mark. The threats of retrenchment make it imperative to develop appropriate data and criteria upon which administrators can make decisions in their efforts to enhance the efficiency and effectiveness of social policy.

Conceptually, the solution is simple. The most effective programs should be continued or expanded and the least effective should be axed. Regrettably, legislators and administrators find that the necessary data are almost never in existence and whatever evaluations are available are rarely, if ever, definitive. Despite the pressing demand for useable program evaluations, they are not forthcoming. Necessity may be the mother of invention, but it cannot create the supply when serious conceptual and technical obstacles are in the way.

OBSTACLES TO THE USE OF EVALUATIONS

Administrative, substantive, and methodological problems continually stand in the way of evaluators charged with reviewing social initiatives. The administrative problems are a product of bureaucratic in-fighting, turf protection, and power politics, while the substantive and methodological difficulties are inherent in the nature of social programs.

The principal administrative obstacles stem from the unwillingness of program officials and employees to have critical performance data publicized. Controlling access to information about program operations and results prevents meddling by outsiders, be they professors, representatives of the public, or legislators who are responsible for the appropriation of funds to continue the effort. Another administrative dilemma arises in choosing an evaluator. Depending on the purpose an evaluation must serve, the product might be needed to provide a timely report, reflect an outside opinion, serve as a diagnostic tool, or bring in new elements of quantitative rigor. No single evaluation can serve all purposes.

Agreeing on standards for measuring program accomplishments presents a tremendous substantive problem. Progress is difficult to measure when the destination is hazy and the start of the journey unmarked. The direction of social efforts is seldom straightforward, and unclear legislative mandates usually muddle it further.

A chronic methodological impediment to objective evaluation is the difficulty of obtaining control data. Controlled social experimentation can be prohibitively expensive, ethically untenable or an inadequate guide to efforts on a national scale. Without control groups though, an evaluation can draw only limited conclusions about the net impact of a program.

Evaluators encounter other methodological barriers when they try to determine how effectively resources are being used in different program approaches. Benefit-cost and cost-effectiveness methodologies are vulnerable, first, because of their reliance on the efficiency criterion in evaluating expenditures. The question "Who benefits from social spending?" is indeed as important as "Does society experience any net gains?" Measurement problems associated with these approaches also compound the methodological difficulties that plague social evaluations. The simple benefit/cost paradigm is made grossly deficient by the presence of a host of non-quantifiable, non-measurable costs and benefits. The models are either burdened with explicit qualifications or ignore so many important variables as to be useless, representing nothing more than hollow exercises and intellectual games.

Given the inherent impediments, the question arises whether the assessment of social programs can help to contribute to the design of sound public policy. Military hardware evaluators can unequivocally test the destructive capability of a weapon system. But social programs cannot be assessed as precisely since the essential criteria are not always readily observed or measured. Contrariwise, in social program assessment, there is a tendency to attach excessive importance to criteria which *can* be measured. It is frequently difficult to specify program objectives and it is equally hard to track down all program effects, for the latter spread out like waves in attenuating circles. Hence, the more thorough and conscientious an evaluation, the less likely is it to yield sharp, definitive conclusions. As one critic has remarked, "the obstacles to scientific evaluation of retraining programs are fundamental and serious. Even a well-conceived and executed study . . . does not make a convincing case that training programs affect employment at all."[1] The criticism, to be sure, is no more "scientific" than the claims of achievements made by program advocates.

Methodologists trying to promote quantitative techniques have discovered how elusive certainty or even objectivity can be with a model that does not adequately reflect reality. Supposedly objective studies of vocational rehabilitation programs have produced ratios of benefits to costs ranging from less than 1 to nearly 100. Other evaluations of the same program and data have reported variations in ratios of more than 40 percent, depending on the choice of discount rate—an issue which is itself subject to an endless debate without any clear resolution. "Rigorous" analyses of Job Corps data have yielded similarly confusing results.[2]

The other side of the coin shows that when the evidence of success or failure is clear and convincing, the matter is already self-evident. Evaluators do not make their observations in a vacuum or from a unique vantage point. They often rely on operational data already known to program administrators. A resounding success or failure does not go unnoticed unless program officials are engaged in a full-scale cover-up or opponents are indifferent to the effects associated with the program, an unlikely occurrence in either case. The on-the-job

1. Robert E. Hall, "Prospects for Shifting the Phillips Curve Through Manpower Policy," *Brookings Papers on Economic Activity* (Washington: The Brookings Institution, 1971), p. 678.

2. Sar A. Levitan and Robert Taggart, *Jobs for the Disabled* (Baltimore: The Johns Hopkins Press, 1977); and Sar A. Levitan and Benjamin Johnston, *The Job Corps* (Baltimore: The Johns Hopkins Press, 1975).

training component of employment and training programs was a clear success; officials knew that before the evaluators presented their airtight case. The evaluations were important to indicate the dimensions of success and provide some explanations for it, but the success surprised no one who was familiar with the program.[3] The contribution of evaluation in that kind of situation is incremental.

THE LIMITED EFFECTS OF EVALUATION

Most evaluations have, at best, only modest effects on the development or refinement of policies and the implementation and administration of programs. The degree of agreement between evaluation findings and prevailing policy is often the most important determinant of how findings are regarded. Institutional and political inertia, manifested in the form of traditional values and long-standing policies, exerts a powerful influence upon the impact of an evaluation. An evaluation of a popular program that can be used to justify additional appropriations has more "impact" than one that criticizes it. The converse is also true: when an unpopular program is a liability to an administration, a critical evaluation may become a convenient rationale for action—the straw that breaks the camel's back. In short, existing values and interests, more than anything else, dictate the ultimate impact of social program evaluations.

The Job Corps experience is illustrative. This program was a controversial, albeit small, piece of the Great Society mosaic. It represented a comprehensive effort to provide a second chance to deficiently educated, unskilled youth from debilitating homes and poverty backgrounds. A thorough and expensive program, it captured much of the driving spirit of the Great Society's efforts. The Job Corps was an experimental program involving a host of unknown variables. It was assessed from its much ballyhooed beginnings, and the evaluators reached as many conclusions as there were studies. The decisions to continue the Job Corps were

---

3. National Council on Employment Policy, "The Impact of Employment and Training Programs" (Washington: The Council, November 1976).

based, to some extent, upon these evaluations, but to a larger extent upon the conviction that the program was moving in the right direction and would show later returns. And as long as no viable alternative emerged, the antipoverty warriors clung to the Job Corps concept.

The Nixon administration, relying on the same studies, cut the Job Corps drastically. But new factors were at work. Nixon had made the Job Corps an issue in his presidential campaign, contending that Job Corps enrollees could take their destiny into their own hands. No evaluation could muster convincing evidence against that contention, which was taken, therefore, as prima facie evidence of the program's failure.

Follow Through is a useful example of the conflicts that arise when program results and policy disagree. As a compensatory preschool program for children from impoverished homes, its purpose was to serve as a follow-up to Head Start, retaining the gains that Head Start children made but then lost in traditional classroom settings. Despite the good grades that Follow Through received in repeated evaluations, both Presidents Nixon and Ford wanted the program cut—and succeeded. Policy had once again preempted observation.

An even more apparent case where evaluations were planned and used to support administration policy involved the housing programs in the early 1970s.[4] After adopting a policy drastically curtailing federal support, the Nixon administration prepared an evaluation of the previously existing programs, apparently to provide an intellectual basis for the administration position. The Congressional Research Service responded with a critique charging that the administration report failed to present clear evidence of either the program's success or failure and could not justify the administration's drastic action.[5]

---

4. U.S. Department of Housing and Urban Development, *Housing in the Seventies* (Washington: Government Printing Office, 1973).

5. Henry Schechter, *Critique of "Housing in the Seventies,"* report prepared by the Congressional Research Service for the U.S. Congress, Senate Committee on Banking, Housing, and Urban Affairs (Washington: Government Printing Office, February 22, 1974).

These head-on conflicts clearly represented more than heated exchanges of assertions. In both, evaluation methodologies were founded on preconceived notions that affected the results. Under circumstances such as those, the very phrasing of the question to be investigated may affect the conclusions of the evaluation. In assessing a social program, one possible hypothesis is that it works, requiring contrary evidence of failure. The converse hypothesis would assume failure in the absence of proof of effectiveness. Using the same evidence, dissimilar results can be obtained from the two hypotheses, because different evaluation standards may be utilized when measurements are imprecise, goals indeterminate, and proofs equivocal. If clear evidence of success is demanded to discount an assumption of failure, a positive verdict is unlikely; if absolute failure must be demonstrated to alter the assumption of success, a positive judgment is inevitable.

THE EVALUATOR'S ROLE

The inherent limitations of evaluations notwithstanding, many practitioners continue to promote their trade as an integral policy tool and a few zealots will pronounce it a panacea. In an effort to stimulate and expand evaluation, the Office of Management and Budget tried to prod federal agencies ". . . to systematically analyze Federal programs (or their components) to determine the extent to which the programs have achieved (or are achieving) their objectives."[6] The directive added that "program evaluation should be undertaken for the express purpose of providing timely, relevant, accurate information concerning program performance that is oriented to a policy or program-related decision."[7] This meant that the justification of program evaluations would rest heavily upon the changes and improvements attributable to them.

The exhortation did not produce the desired results. However, it did reflect the confusion and frustration of pinning down the role of evaluation. The OMB fiat took a simplistic approach to a complex problem. Program evaluation has broader objectives

---

6. "Evaluation Management: A Background Paper," U.S. Office of Management and Budget, May 1975, p. 2.

7. *Ibid.,* p. vi.

than "bottom line" answers. It is inextricably associated with program operations and policy analysis under conditions that cannot be uniformly and neatly defined.

At congressional oversight and appropriations hearings, inquiries are frequently raised about the success of evaluation. Evaluators respond with "cause and effect" examples of where evaluation made a difference. These purported examples of evaluations influencing specific policy or program decisions are practically limitless when an appropriation committee has to be convinced. Considering the premium put on the "relevance" of findings, evaluation managers are only too happy to find cases justifying their work.

However, evaluating evaluations is a hazardous pastime that can quickly run afoul of the same methodological problems plaguing evaluations of social programs. The central problem, analogous to the control data problem, is to determine what would have happened if an evaluation had not been done. The selection of control groups made up of individual efforts is difficult and makes the study of contrasting effects of evaluations and non-evaluations on bureaucratic and political behavior extremely frustrating. In practice, the process of assessing the impact of evaluations is no more than a guessing game. Like the claims of social policy framers, allegations about the usefulness of evaluation, by those who conduct and sponsor it, reflect optimism more than valid evidence.

Discounting vested claims it remains doubtful what a satisfactory norm would actually be, even if the precise impact of evaluations could be measured. Few evaluators believe that their findings should be the only basis of program and policy decisions. A former Department of Labor official responsible for evaluation cautioned that there is no single, correct assessment, but rather that different evaluations will employ "different methodologies, different data sets, different political approaches. Everyone has a bias regardless of how well or rigorously trained he is." Because the process of assimilation is usually slow and subtle, ". . . evidence has its effect through a gathering of a preponderant weight of information. . . ."[8] Another evaluator, a former HEW Assistant Secretary for Planning and Evaluation, suggested:

> Other ingredients are politics, value judgments, management and other data, situational factors (are there in fact live alternatives?), considered reasoning, common sense, and, on occasion, use of systematic analysis techniques such as simulation.[9]

Evaluations cannot be the only "facts" bearing on decisions because the available methodologies are not—and will never be—sophisticated enough to capture *all* the relevant variables.

Some evaluators sensitive to questions about the relevance of their work to policy formulation have tried to gear it better to the needs of officials. But in doing this, they have run the risk of filling an information void with misinformation. The number of cases in which the impact of an evaluation was justified by its findings can probably be matched by an equal number in which the impact was greater than the findings warranted.

This phenomenon has been viewed by one prominent observer of social programs as evidence of the substantial potential for abuse that exists in taking findings too seriously:

> Evaluation is being used as a decision making tool more than it warrants. . . . To use evaluation results for policy-making . . . we need to be able to separate fact from artifact.[10]

A 1971 evaluation of Head Start by the Westinghouse Learning Corporation and an Ohio University group is an example of an evaluation that had much more impact than either the evaluators

---

8. Interview with Ernst Stromsdorfer, "The Use of Evaluation by Federal Agencies," a Symposium Workshop Conducted by the Mitre Corporation (Washington: The Mitre Corporation, November 1976), pp. 3-4.

9. William A. Morrill and Walton J. Francis, "Evaluation from the HEW Perspective," remarks prepared for the Federal Executive Institute, Workshop in Program Management, Charlottesville, VA, May 3, 1976.

10. Selma J. Mushkin, "Evaluations: Use With Caution," *Evaluation,* Vol. 1, No. 2, 1973, p. 31.

intended or the evaluation warranted. It sought a quick measure of the program's long term effect on its participants. The motives for the evaluation were not clear to all persons involved. Some thought that it "was one of a series of evaluations systematically identified as part of a larger plan." But defenders of the program perceived a plot "to find a way to kill Head Start or to mutilate it."[11] Coupled with the uncertainty about the underlying reasons—if there were any—for the evaluation, were inconsistencies in the choice of objectives it was measuring, the purpose it was going to serve, and alleged shortcomings in the design. The evaluators wanted to measure accomplishments with respect to objectives that the antipoverty officials never considered. The sponsors of the study saw the need for an evaluation that would support a straightforward yes or no decision on program funding. Program officials favored a diagnostic evaluation that would indicate effectiveness and also provide insights as to where and how performance could be improved. Critics attacked the design on methodological grounds.

Yet, in spite of the serious design failures, the shortcomings in the analysis of the program's effectiveness, and the fact that most recommendations did not derive from the evidence collected, the Westinghouse/Ohio evaluation wielded considerable influence by bolstering the biases of program detractors. As early as February 1969, President Nixon began hinting at the poor long term results that preliminary findings were implying. The results were also used to fuel debate about the fate of other antipoverty programs.

> The Westinghouse Report came along at a convenient time to shake confidence in OEO's ability to manage successful programs and to dampen public hope in family or child educational interventions as an effective way to reduce poverty. . . .[12]

In addition to methodological inadequacies, administrative barriers, substantive ambiguities, the underlying presumptions

---

11. Lois-ellin Datta, "The Impact of the Westinghouse/Ohio Evaluation on the Development of Project Head Start," in *The Evaluation of Social Programs,* Clark Abt, editor (Beverly Hills, CA: Sage Publications, 1977), pp. 131-132.

12. *Ibid.,* pp. 160-161.

and biases of evaluators, and the preferences of policymakers, the impact of evaluations can also be negatively affected by unrealistic expectations about what can be proved. Expectations are raised because of the success of program evaluation and related techniques for systematic analysis outside the social sciences. Policymakers and program officials, encountering difficulties in making their own assessments of program effectiveness, grasp at straws, in the hope of greater success from "scientific" evaluation. But unlike military hardware development, space exploration, or biomedical testing and research, government social programs possess a large central element of human behavior that renders their results unpredictable and rapidly changeable. They are crude and uncertain interventions into complex social and historical developments. Yet in spite of the dissimilarities between the physical and social worlds, expectations persist that evaluators of social programs can achieve the same precision as laboratory scientists.

To paraphrase Phillip B. Crosby: Evaluation has much in common with sex. "Everyone is for it (under certain conditions, of course). Everyone feels they understand it (even though they wouldn't want to explain it). Everyone thinks execution is only a matter of following natural inclinations."[13]

IT'S NOT PERFECT, BUT . . .

The inherent difficulties imply a great sense of uncertainty in evaluations of social programs. That is no reason to stop evaluations, but they should be viewed with a degree of skepticism and used with a degree of caution. Even persuasive findings do not simplify decisions and certainly do not eliminate debate. But evaluation remains necessary and helpful. Indeed, policymakers must determine which programs to support, to modify, and to discontinue, and they need relevant information that will help them make sensible decisions. This calls for the continuing collection of relevant data and their analysis.

---

13. Phillip B. Crosby, *Quality is Free* (New York: McGraw Hill, 1979), cited in *Business Week,* March 12, 1979, p. 10.

Those who sponsor, prepare, or use evaluations should not delude themselves that government decisions can be made on purely objective, "scientific" grounds. In the final analysis, they rest on personal judgments, no matter how many statistics are furnished and how good they may be. The 19th century British economist Henry Clay said that statistics are no substitute for judgment. His admonition is as true today as a century ago.

Index